TURNING POINTS

By Donna Reynolds

THE SALEM WITCH TRIALS

Cavendish Square

New York

Published in 2021 by Cavendish Square Publishing, LLC
243 5th Avenue, Suite 136, New York, NY 10016

First Edition

Portions of this work were originally authored by Don Nardo and published as *The Salem Witch Trials* (*American History*). All new material this edition authored by Donna Reynolds.

All websites were available and accurate when this book was sent to press.

Cataloging-in-Publication Data

Names: Reynolds, Donna.
Title: The Salem witch trials / Donna Reynolds.
Description: First edition. | New York : Cavendish Square, 2021. | Series: Turning points | Includes index.
Identifiers: ISBN 9781502657718 (pbk.) | ISBN 9781502657725 (library bound) | ISBN 9781502657732 (ebook)
Subjects: LCSH: Trials (Witchcraft)–Massachusetts–Salem–Juvenile literature. | Witchcraft–Massachusetts–Salem–History–Juvenile literature.
Classification: LCC KFM2478.8.W5 R468 2021 | DDC 345.744'50288–dc23

Editor: Jennifer Lombardo
Copy Editor: Michelle Denton
Designer: Deanna Paternostro

CPSIA compliance information: Batch #CS20CSQ: For further information contact Cavendish Square Publishing LLC, New York, New York, at 1-877-980-4450.

Printed in the United States of America

TABLE OF CONTENTS

INTRODUCTION

A MISUNDERSTOOD EVENT

People began settling in Salem, a village in Massachusetts, around the 1620s. By the 1690s, this village was primarily made up of Puritans. The Puritan religion, which seems strict by modern-day Christian standards, taught that the Bible needed to be interpreted literally and applied to everyday life. Puritans tended to wear simply made clothes to avoid the sins of greed and pride, and they frowned upon behaviors such as dancing, playing games, or reading things that didn't center on religion. In such a strict environment, being different could be dangerous.

One day in January 1692, two young girls in the community began exhibiting strange behavior, including seizure-like fits and screaming outbursts. The community was not medically advanced, however, and these behaviors resulted in severe confusion and misunderstanding. A local doctor believed the explanation for the behavior was that a witch had put a spell on the girls to cause them physical suffering. Several other young girls in the community began to exhibit the same symptoms, and all blamed it on witches. They began to accuse specific people, which sparked a witch hunt. As a result, 20 people were executed, more died in jail, and countless lives were ruined.

This engraving of a Puritan wedding showcases the somber clothing and attitudes of this particular religious group.

FROM THE SOURCE: THE MALLEUS MALEFICARUM

To reinforce the Christian religion's tough stance against witches, two German Dominican monks published the *Malleus Maleficarum*, or *The Hammer of Witches*, in 1487. This volume listed the supernatural acts performed by witches and told how witches caused disease, destroyed crops, and kidnapped and ate children. More women than men were witches, the book said, because women were naturally wicked and too weak to resist the temptation of witchcraft. At the time, women were seen as inferior, or worse than, men in almost every area of society.

The following passage from the *Malleus Maleficarum* explains typical beliefs at that time, which have since been disproven:

> *Now the wickedness of women is spoken of in [the Bible, which says that] ... all wickedness is but little to the wickedness of a woman ... [W]omen are naturally more impressionable, and more ready to receive the influence of a disembodied spirit ... they have slippery tongues, and are unable to conceal from their fellow women those things which by evil arts they know; and, since they are weak, they find an easy and secret manner of vindicating themselves by witchcraft ... We may add ... that since they are feebler both in mind and body, it is not surprising that they should come more under the spell of witchcraft.*[1]

Monks were among the few educated people in Europe at that time. Citizens tended to assume that a book written by monks and approved by the pope must be both righteous and factual. Because of this preconceived notion, most people didn't question the things the *Malleus Maleficarum* said.

1. Heinrich Kramer and James Sprenger, *The Malleus Maleficarum*, trans. Montague Summers (New York, NY: Cosimo Classics, 2007), pp. 43–44, books.google.com/books?id=bbLe57H2GcUC&printsec=frontcover#v=onepage&q&f=false.

According to the Bible, witchcraft involves asking demons for help to cast evil spells on others. In 1484, Pope Innocent VIII had released an edict, or announcement, stating that witches definitely existed, so at the time of the Salem witch trials, a majority of people in Europe and its recently founded colonies in North America were convinced that witches were real—and that it was their duty as Christians to kill them.

To understand how an entire community could fall victim to such mass hysteria, we must first look at the beliefs and teachings of those who were in power in these times. Their words were taken very seriously and almost always blindly obeyed.

The Witch Trials Today

Once the hysteria surrounding the witch trials settled down, many people in Salem began to see that the event had been blown out of proportion. For decades, it was considered an embarrassing chapter in American history; according to historian Danny Lewis, people in Salem preferred to pretend it had never happened and refused to talk about it. However, this changed in the 20th century for several reasons.

One major reason was a shift in the way people viewed witches. Instead of seeing them as evil people who were doing the work of the devil, society began to view them as fun and quirky. In additon, Wicca, a religion that uses witchcraft as a way to worship various gods, goddesses, and nature, was developed in 1954 and has grown in popularity since then. However, Wiccans don't practice witchcraft the way it was described in the *Malleus Maleficarum* or the Bible. Instead, they believe that by using certain herbs, stones, and other natural items, they can cast spells to influence the world around them. For example, a modern-day witch might cast a spell to try to improve their chances of getting a promotion at work.

In addition to real people calling themselves witches, fantasy witches became popular in the media. According to the website Vox, the 1960s TV show *Bewitched* marked a turning point in how people saw the Salem witch trials and the town of Salem itself. The show, which features a witch named Samantha who can do powerful magic simply by twitching her nose, was extremely popular and led to a cultural fascination with witches. In need of money, the town of Salem decided to capitalize on this fascination by promoting "witch tourism," even though the witch trials originally took place in a small town several miles away. At the time, it was called Salem Village; today, it is known as Danvers.

While this move did indeed revitalize Salem, it has also led to a warped view of history, with many important details obscured.

Shown here are witches participating in a public magic ritual in Salem on October 31, 2018. The event, which was called the Salem Witches' Magic Circle, was held to honor the spirits of people who had died.

The witch trials were a tragic time of mass hysteria in which many innocent people were killed, yet Salem has become a destination for all things witchy and is especially popular around Halloween. People began to put forth the idea that the women who were killed were martyrs (people killed because of their religion), targeted for secretly practicing Wicca. However, since they were Puritans who believed strongly in the Bible, this is highly unlikely. According to Vox,

> *Those two strands of historical narrative—Salem as a site of mass panic, and Salem as witch city—are factually opposed to each other. Kristina Stevick, artistic director of the Cry Innocent project, which lets people experience a mock witch trial, thinks it's utterly illogical. "A person can't both be innocent and a martyr. That narrative really puzzles me."*[1]

In part because of this view of the accused as martyrs, the way people talk about the witch trials has changed. One example of this in popular culture is the Halloween classic *Hocus Pocus*, in which one of the first scenes shows three sisters who are witches being killed in Salem after kidnapping a child and stealing her soul. While this movie is fun to watch, it's important to remember that it's fiction and that no one who was killed in the witch trials could fly on broomsticks or turn people into cats.

Because of these preconceived notions, many people think they know what happened in Salem in the 1690s and are unwilling to learn the true story. This can be dangerous because, as Stevick pointed out, "ultimately developing a more complex understanding of history is necessary if one is to avoid repeating it."[2]

CHAPTER ONE

SETTING THE STAGE

Since the witch trials occurred, many people have put forth suggestions as to why they happened, but many of these suggestions are relatively simplistic, focusing on only one explanation. For example, many people think the Puritans' superstition made it easier for them to fall prey to mass hysteria rather than thinking logically. Although this theory ignores many other factors that were in play at the time, the Puritans' beliefs certainly played a large role; after all, if they didn't accept witches as real, no one would have been put on trial for witchcraft.

Fleeing Persecution

The religious sect that came to be known as Puritanism emerged from the turmoil surrounding the early years of the Church of England. Before the 16th century, England, like other European lands, was a Catholic country that, in religious matters, recognized the authority of the pope in Rome. That situation changed quite suddenly and drastically in the 1530s. When the religious authorities in Rome refused to grant King Henry VIII a divorce, he angrily and boldly separated his country from the established church. The result was the formation of the Church of England, a Protestant denomination of Christianity.

Puritans opposed the Church of England, which was established by Henry VIII (*shown here*). Because they were persecuted for their beliefs, many of them left England and came to what is now the United States.

As time went on, the English monarchs and most of their subjects felt that their new church satisfactorily met their needs. However, a few of the more devout inhabitants of the country were not so happy with the new religious climate. They came to view the new church as too liberal and permissive. Because they desired to purify the church by taking it back to stricter, more fundamental Christian ideas and customs, they became known as Puritans.

It is not surprising that the Puritans quickly earned a reputation as troublemakers, especially to the reigning monarchs and high-ranking church leaders. In the early 1600s, these leaders began to persecute the Puritans. In response, some Puritans crossed the Atlantic Ocean in 1620 and established a colony at Plymouth, in what is now southern Massachusetts. The Plymouth Puritans, as well as others who traveled with them to the New World for economic reasons, came to be known as the Pilgrims. Not long after the landfall at Plymouth, other Puritans arrived and settled in an area further north on the Massachusetts coast. In 1628, John Endecott, a Puritan leader, came to this northern area with about 60 followers and founded Salem, which grew into an important town in the large, new Massachusetts Bay Colony. Other Puritans were soon drawn to this new North American outpost.

Rising Tensions

Also established in the Massachusetts Bay Colony during this period was Salem Village, a separate entity from Salem Town. Located along the coast, Salem Town was a bustling port with a number of shops, large merchants' houses, and local government buildings. In contrast, Salem Village—which is now the small town of Danvers—consisted of a few scattered farms and farmhouses roughly clustered around the village center, which had only a few buildings in it.

Salem Village was so far from its nearest neighbor, Salem Town, that it took several hours to walk from one to the other. Along the way, travelers had to cross several small rivers and inlets. At first, this difficult trip presented a major physical challenge to the residents of Salem Village. Before the meetinghouse was built in the village center in 1672, every Sunday they had to walk all the way to the church in Salem Town and back again.

FROM THE SOURCE: PURITAN BELIEFS

One major factor in the witch trials was the Puritans' strongly held belief that the Christian God clearly and observably intervened in human affairs. Anything good that happened was attributed to God's actions, while anything bad that happened was attributed to the devil. Sometimes this reasoning was used to justify views and actions that harmed others, as in the case of the witch trials or relations with local Native Americans. This is illustrated in this excerpt from a letter written by John Winthrop, the first governor of the Massachusetts Bay Colony, describing life in Boston in 1634:

> *That you are pleased among yr many & weighty imployments to spend so many serious thought and good wishes upon us, & the work of the Lord in our hands, I must needs acknowledge it among other the special favours of God towards us ... I esteem them [the residents of Boston] to be in all about 4000 souls & upward: in good health ... so as (through the Lords special providence) there hath not died about 2: or 3: grown persons, & about so many Children all in the last year ... For the natives, they are near all dead of the smallpox, so the Lord hath cleared our title to what we possess.*[1]

1. John Winthrop to Nathaniel Rich, May 22, 1634, Gilder Lehrman Institute of American History, www.gilderlehrman.org/sites/default/files/inline-pdfs/t-01105_0.pdf.

This initial reliance on the church and other facilities in the town was not the only source of frustration to the inhabitants of Salem Village. For a long time, they had little say in running their village, which fell under the legal and political jurisdiction of Salem Town. The leaders of the town taxed the villagers and set the prices for crops and other items exported from the village to the town.

This 1879 map shows how far Salem Village (now Danvers) was from Salem Town (now simply Salem). Both were far from Boston, so officials who lived there had very little idea of what was going on during the witch trials.

The town's elders also appointed the village's constable and controlled the distribution of land parcels and the building of roads in the village.

This situation led to an intense social rivalry that was another contributing factor to the witch trials. The wealthy Porters who lived in the village had connections with people of high social standing in Salem Town and therefore supported the village's continued reliance on the town. The Putnams, in contrast, were less wealthy and supported greater independence for the village. This rivalry was generally split along geographic lines, as people on the east side had access to better farmland and didn't have as far to travel to Salem Town and the markets there. According to *Encyclopedia Britannica*, because of these social tensions, "Squabbles over property were commonplace, and litigiousness [taking people to court] was rampant."[1]

These tensions deepened when a man named Samuel Parris was appointed as the reverend of Salem in 1689. At that time, reverends were paid by their congregation and lived in a house called a parsonage that was owned by the town. When one reverend left, the next would be given the use of the parsonage. Parris demanded a higher salary than most reverends as well as permanent ownership of the parsonage, which outraged some of the villagers. Furthermore, instead of remaining neutral and trying to calm the existing tensions, Parris ended up making them worse. According to the book *The New England Soul*,

> *Parris inflamed local rivalries by declaring that "if ever there were witches, Men and Women in covenant with the Devil, here are multitudes in New-England." By March 1692, he was convinced that witches had infiltrated the churches, including his own Salem congregation … Such preaching offered a powerful and dangerous release for social and political tensions that had been brewing throughout the previous decades. It encouraged the villagers to purge their feelings of frustration and guilt by locating and destroying "witches" in their midst. In many cases these witches were individuals who had run afoul of Parris and his key clan of supporters, the Putnam family.*[2]

HISTORY HAPPENED HERE: DANVERS, MASSACHUSETTS

In 1752, Salem Village gained its independence from Salem Town and changed its name to Danvers. Today, more than 12 historical houses are preserved in the town, many of which are associated with the mass hysteria of the witch trials. For instance, the Putnam house still stands, although a lack of funds has prevented it from being fully restored. Modern-day Salem has capitalized far more on the history of the witch trials than Danvers has.

Parris's assertion that witches were living among the villagers of Salem was a key factor in the hysteria that followed. Puritan society vigorously promoted a simple existence and frequent worship of God. Anyone who deviated from these rules was viewed with suspicion, and the perpetrator was subject to public punishment. Among the common sins and crimes were failing to attend church, kissing in public, breaking an engagement to be married, and disagreeing with community leaders on any matter. One common punishment was to be tied to a post and whipped. Another was to sit for hours or days in the stocks, which were wooden frameworks that trapped a person's hands, feet, and head. The harshest punishment was death, which was generally by hanging. This is how 19 of the 20 accused witches who were condemned to be executed in Salem met their untimely end.

The strictness of Puritan laws and customs relating to religious worship was matched by the harsh manner in which society treated many of its members.

Shown here is an illustration of the punishment of being pilloried, or put in the stocks. This device was often in a central location such as a town square so that, in addition to the physical pain of having to stand in such a position for hours, the person being punished would be seen by all their neighbors and be embarrassed.

The Puritans openly practiced what today are recognized as serious forms of discrimination and abuse. In general, society catered to the young, the strong, the wealthy, and the male. Women were seen as inferior, as were poor people, most elderly people, people of color, and people with disabilities. Children born with severe birth defects were often viewed as the devil's offspring. Gender and class discrimination even invaded the church, where the wealthiest people got the best seats (in front, closest to the pulpit) and men and women sat in separate sections.

Knowing all of these facts about life in Salem Village, it's clearly no coincidence that the first person to be accused of witchcraft was a slave named Tituba who occasionally practiced folk magic. Records don't indicate what religion Tituba followed, but as a slave

THEY MADE HISTORY: SAMUEL PARRIS

Samuel Parris was born in 1653 in London, England, but soon after his birth, his father bought a sugar plantation in Barbados and moved the family there. When his father died in 1673, Parris left Harvard University in Cambridge, Massachusetts, to go back to Barbados and take over the plantation. It was in Barbados that he bought his two slaves, a married couple named Tituba and John Indian. Being unsuccessful in business, he moved back to Massachusetts in 1680 with his two slaves, started a family, and gave up business to become a minister. In July 1689, thanks to the influence of the Putnam family, he officially accepted the position of reverend in Salem Village, where he became embroiled in the conflicts that were already happening and further divided the town. He was a prominent part of the Salem witch trials; in fact, some people have gone so far as to blame him for the entire event, although most historians note that the incident was far too complicated to be blamed on one person.

This depiction of Tituba illustrates the racist way she was viewed by her community. This racism made her an easy target for accusations.

who had been kidnapped from a village in South America and sent to Barbados before being purchased and brought to Massachusetts, it's quite possible that she wasn't a Christian, let alone a Puritan. This fact alone would have made her a target, but combined with her foreign heritage, dark skin, and low social status, she would have been one of the most vulnerable people in Salem Village.

Oppression of Women

The view of women in the late 1600s as inferior to men was yet another factor in the Salem witch trials. Many people inaccurately believe that it was the main or even only factor, but in reality, it was this in combination with the social and political tensions that created an explosive situation.

At this point in history, women weren't allowed to vote or publicly disagree with men. As one essay pointed out:

> *While those girls who took on the role of victim likely did not do so entirely to further the political agendas of their parents, it is clear that being afflicted by witches during the Salem Witch Trials provided a unique opportunity for those with little to no political or social power to gain attention and authority overnight. One must simply act the part of a victim, pose accusations against others, and reap the benefits. As these benefits were attractive and plainly visible, it is no wonder that so many young women and girls became involved in the Trials.*[3]

In addition to mainly being the accusers, women were mainly the accused. Many people today believe this is because Puritans thought only women could be witches, but in reality, they believed people of any gender could practice witchcraft. The truth is that women of the time were far more vulnerable than men, so they were much easier to accuse. There were also far stricter behavioral standards for women than for men, so it was easier for women than for men to stray from the accepted path and have their actions be seen as proof of witchcraft.

All of these various factors combined to create an atmosphere that not only supported but amplified the hysteria that followed the first accusations of witchcraft. What might easily have been

PAST MEETS PRESENT: MODERN "WITCH HUNTS"

Today, most people are aware that witches as described in the Bible don't exist and that the people who were accused in 1692 were innocent. However, the term "witch hunt" has survived and today is used to describe a situation where people who are innocent of something are being targeted and accused, often for political reasons. Sometimes this term is used accurately; for example, in the 1950s, fear of communism caused Senator Joseph McCarthy to lead a witch hunt for communists living in the United States. Most people who were accused had never been members of the American Communist Party, but even if they were acquitted in a trial, they were almost always socially shunned. Many people lost their jobs and social connections as a result of such accusations.

Other times, people use the term "witch hunt" when they feel unfairly accused of something. For example, some people have called the #MeToo movement a witch hunt because they feel that some of the men who have been accused of inappropriate behavior have had their actions blown out of proportion. Many men have also expressed fears that they'll unknowingly make themselves the next target. However, others have argued that the only men accused are the ones who have behaved inappropriately.

contained in another time or place spiraled out of control in Salem, leading to the deaths of 20 innocent people.

How You See History

1. How did the various causes of the Salem witch trials interact to create an atmosphere of fear and suspicion?
2. What kinds of benefits might someone get from accusing another person of witchcraft?
3. Describe a modern situation not mentioned in this book that could be described as a metaphorical witch hunt.

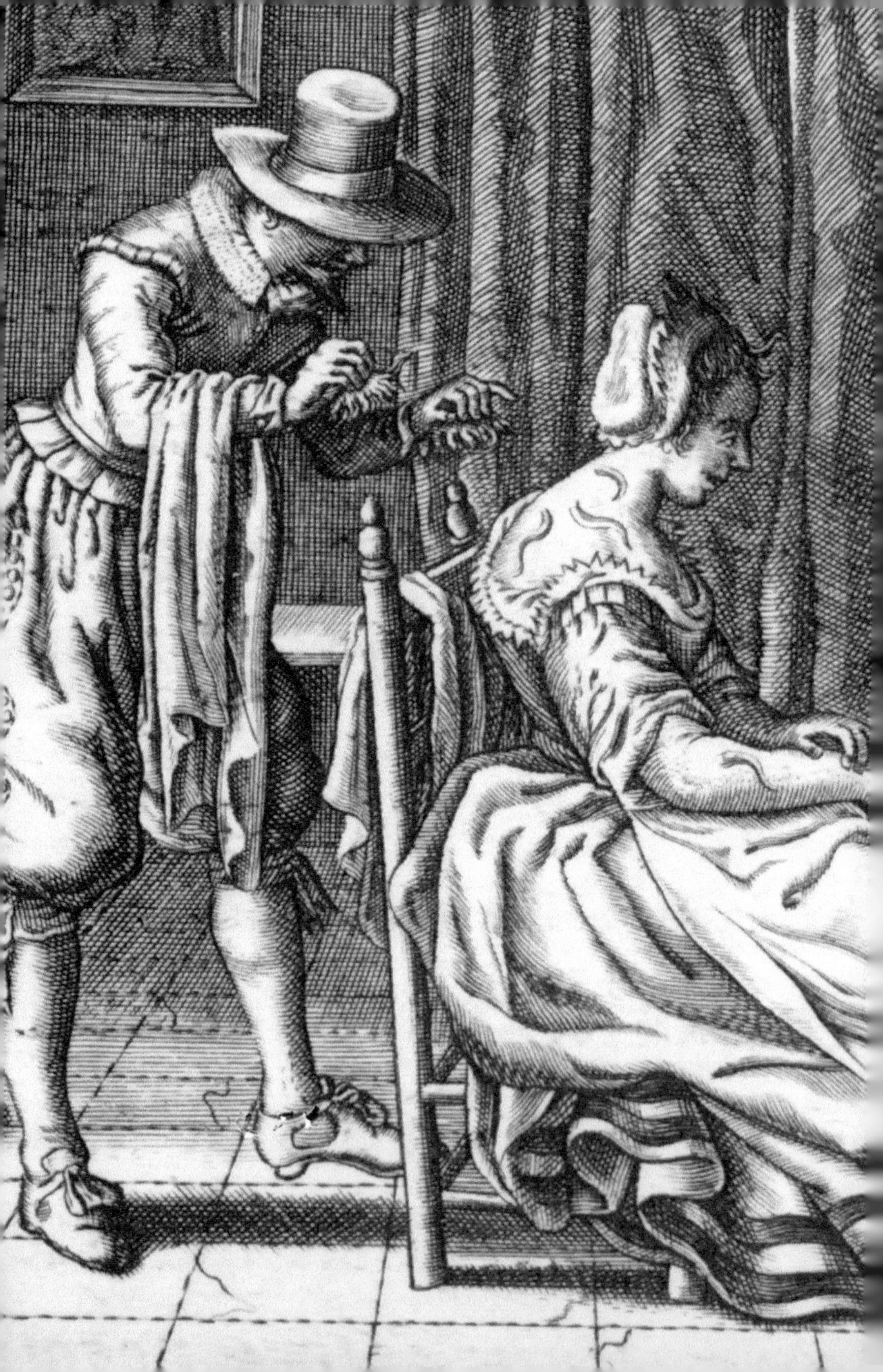

CHAPTER TWO

THE INCIDENTS START

In the late 1600s, the study of medicine was practically nonexistent. While most settlements had at least one doctor, there were no medical schools in the colonies at that time, so their knowledge generally wasn't good enough to accurately diagnose and treat most illnesses. Many physical and mental ailments, especially in religious communities, were believed to be caused by demonic possession, and bloodletting—the practice of draining the patient of some of their blood—was the most common treatment for any illness. Unfortunately, this "treatment" often made the condition worse. With this in mind, it's understandable that the witch trials started with reports of an unidentifiable illness.

A Historical Precedent

The Salem witch trials were not the earliest recorded arrest and execution of a colonial Puritan for witchcraft. Ann Hibbins of Boston was the sister of a colonial governor, Richard Bellingham, and the wife of a prominent merchant, William Hibbins. Unfortunately for Ann, she earned a reputation for having a temper and speaking her mind, which Puritans believed were unholy traits. In particular, she was penalized on several occasions for raising her voice to and arguing with men.

◀ Putting bloodsucking leeches on a patient's body, as shown here, was one method of bloodletting—a common medical treatment in colonial times.

HISTORY HAPPENED HERE: VARDØ, NORWAY

Witch hunts were not exclusive to the American colonies. In fact, Europe had a much longer history of this brutal practice. This is where the idea of burning witches at the stake comes from; that was how many people were executed for witchcraft in European countries, while most of those accused in Salem were hanged.

The small, coastal Norwegian village of Vardø has been named the Witch Capital of Norway because of the fact that 140 witch trials were held there between 1593 and 1692. In total, 91 people were found guilty and burned or tortured to death. This high number was partially due to Norway's cold climate and frequent storms, which sometimes claimed the lives of fishermen and were often blamed on witches at the time. On June 23, 2011, Vardø revealed a monument to its witch trial victims on the spot where it is believed the victims were executed. According to *Norwegian American*, the memorial "was designed to draw visitors to an economically depressed yet exceptionally beautiful area of Norway ... [It] is also a part of the modern trend to apologize and atone for injustices of [the] past and to grant the victims official recognition."[1]

1. "The Evil North: Vardø's Witch Trials," *Norwegian American*, December 28, 2016, www.norwegianamerican.com/heritage/the-evil-north-vardos-witch-trials.

Not long after her husband died in 1654, Ann was arrested following multiple accusations of witchcraft. A jury found her guilty, and she was executed in 1656.

Another witch trial and execution occurred in Hartford, now the capital of the state of Connecticut, six years later. The Hartford witch hunt started when an eight-year-old fell ill and "in her delirium, she cried out that a neighbor had afflicted her."[1] The unknown

The small, isolated town of Vardø was once the site of many of witch trials and executions.

illness killed her, and her parents, as well as some of the neighbors, blamed witchcraft. Around the same time, a girl named Ann Cole exhibited strange physical symptoms. Increase Mather, a prominent Puritan minister, described them by writing,

> *She was and is accounted a person of real Piety and Integrity. Nevertheless, in the Year 1662 … She was taken with very*

strange Fits, wherein her Tongue was [caused] by a [demon] to express things which she her self knew nothing of.[2]

Several locals were named as the suspects in these cases: Nathaniel and Rebecca Greensmith, Elizabeth Seager, Andrew and Mary Sanford, William Ayres, Judith Varlett, and James Walkley. Some of the people in this group already had a bad reputation in town. For example, the Greensmiths, who lived next door to Ann Cole, were

FROM THE SOURCE: A CONFESSION OF WITCHCRAFT

No one knows why, but Rebecca Greensmith admitted in court to being a witch. According to the two ministers who questioned her,

> *She (Rebecca) forthwith and freely confessed those things to be true, that she (and other persons named in the discourse) had familiarity with the devil. Being asked whether she had made an express covenant with him, she answered she had not, only as she promised to go with him when he called (which she had accordingly done several times) ...*
>
> *She also declared that the devil first appeared to her in the form of a deer or fawn, skipping about her, wherewith she was not much affrighted but by degrees he contrived talk with her, and that their meetings were frequently at such a place, (near her own house) that some of the company came in one shape and some in another, and one in particular in the shape of a crow came flying to them.*[1]

1. Quoted in "Colonial Women: Rebecca Greensmith," *History of American Women* (blog), accessed September 11, 2019, www.womenhistoryblog.com/2008/03/rebecca-greensmith.html.

disliked by their neighbors, and Nathaniel had been found guilty of theft twice. Elizabeth Seager had committed such crimes as adultery (cheating on her husband) and blasphemy (speaking badly about her religion). The group often had parties at night that involved dancing. Parties, dancing, and staying up late all went against Puritan teachings and made them prime targets for accusations of witchcraft. In the end, though, only the Greensmiths and another woman named Mary Barnes were formally charged. All three were executed.

What Really Happened?

There was, therefore, ample precedent in New England's Puritan communities for young people's illnesses being blamed on supposed witches, and there were other, previous incidents of witch hunts in Europe in the mid-1600s. Moreover, it's likely no coincidence that the first children to suffer such fits in Salem—Parris's daughter, nine-year-old Elizabeth "Betty" Parris, and his niece, 11-year-old Abigail Williams—lived in the parsonage.

Betty and Abigail spent hours listening to Tituba tell stories about the Caribbean, where she had been sold into slavery. It was only natural for Tituba to include information about magic in these sessions, since both black and white magic were features of Caribbean island culture. (Black magic consisted of spells intended to hurt other people; white magic was thought to bring good fortune or to reveal glimpses of the future.) Thus, the presence of Tituba in the household almost ensured that the children would be exposed to knowledge of the supernatural. Some sources state that Tituba practiced witchcraft herself and taught the girls how to play fortune-telling games, but "there are no references to this in the court records and no evidence that she did this."[3] However, there is some evidence that the girls and their 12-year-old friend, Ann Putnam Jr., started playing fortune-telling games on their own, likely influenced by the stories Tituba had told them.

The exact sequence of events leading from Betty and Abigail's listening to stories with Tituba to the girls' first experiences with seizure-like fits is unclear. Soon, though, other girls in the community started displaying the same symptoms as Betty and Abigail.

Even today, it's unclear exactly what caused the strange behaviors that led to the girls' accusations, although there have been many attempts to figure it out. Most of the modern explanations are complex and involve many factors, and none is completely satisfactory. It may be a combination of two or more of the following explanations.

The most commonly invoked explanation is a combination of mass hysteria—known to mental health professionals as "collective obsessional behavior" or "mass psychogenic illness"—and conversion disorder. Conversion disorder is a mental illness in which, according to medical sociologist Dr. Robert Bartholomew, "psychological conflict and distress are converted into aches and pains that have no physical origin."[4] Some doctors believe mass psychogenic illness is a subcategory of

To the Puritans, fortune-telling was a sin—the start of a slippery slope that ended with conjuring demons. Shown here is a historical illustration of a group of witches dancing with the devil.

PAST MEETS PRESENT: LE ROY, NEW YORK

Blaming witchcraft for unexplained illnesses may be a thing of the past, but mass psychogenic illness is by no means outdated. In fact, according to Simon Wessely, a doctor who specializes in disease patterns and the chairman of the department of psychological medicine at King's College in London, hundreds of outbreaks happen each year in the United States alone. Generally, the symptoms are mild, affect only a small group of people, and pass quickly, so they are rarely noticed. However, one mysterious case made international news in 2012.

In the small town of Le Roy, New York, a few girls started experiencing fits very similar to the ones described during the Salem witch trials. They uncontrollably twitched, yelled, and fainted, and there seemed to be no real cause. The symptoms soon spread to others in the town. Experts tested the soil and water for toxins and found nothing, so a neurologist from Buffalo, New York, came to the conclusion that it was a case of conversion disorder and mass psychogenic illness. Outraged parents and guardians rejected this diagnosis; one compared it to the Salem witch trials by asking, "what are we, living in the 1600s?"[1] Many people were accused of faking their symptoms for media attention. The whole situation bore a striking resemblance to 1690s Salem.

Not everyone affected in Le Roy believed they were suffering from conversion disorder, especially since they didn't feel any more stressed than they had been before symptoms started. One doctor proposed that the main cause was an infection that caused the immune system to change the patients' brain chemistry, but when he was informed that many of the girls had stressful family lives, he said, "I don't know, maybe I'm wrong. It's hard to distinguish between the drug and the placebo effect."[2] In the end, a combination of behavioral therapy, antibiotics, and antidepressants improved the symptoms of most of the affected girls, but just as in Salem, the incident was never satisfactorily explained.

1. Quoted in Susan Dominus, "What Happened to the Girls in Le Roy," *New York Times Magazine*, March 7, 2012, www.nytimes.com/2012/03/11/magazine/teenage-girls-twitching-le-roy.html.

2. Quoted in Dominus, "What Happened to the Girls in Le Roy."

conversion disorder, but others believe they're two separate disorders. Some of the girls who exhibited symptoms were refugees who had lost their homes and loved ones in King William's War, which was fought in New England from 1689 to 1697. Their physical symptoms, some experts say, could have been caused by conversion disorder as a result of the tragedy they had witnessed.

In 2018, a neurologist suggested that instead of conversion disorder, the illness was a rare, little-known autoimmune disease called anti-NMDR encephalitis. Either way, many doctors and historians believe one or more of the girls had a real illness.

In support of the mass psychogenic illness theory, some historians have noted that the girls who showed symptoms had probably heard the story of Ann Cole and may have unconsciously started showing the same symptoms. As some of the girls started showing symptoms, the theory goes, others in the community did as well because the belief that they were being bewitched was so strong that it manifested physically. Although the illness is psychological in origin, the physical symptoms are very real, and most of the time the victim has no idea that what's happening to them is caused by stress.

A second modern-day explanation is ergot poisoning. Ergot is a fungus that grows on grains such as wheat and rye in warm, wet conditions after cold winters—conditions that fit the time period right before the accusations began. It produces a substance called ergotamine, which is similar to the drug lysergic acid diethylamide (LSD). The symptoms of ergot poisoning, or ergotism, are similar to those the affected girls exhibited. However, not everyone agrees that this is a definitive explanation. For one thing, ergotism tends to affect children much more strongly because they need to ingest a much lower amount of ergot than adults to start showing symptoms, and many of the accusers were in their mid- to upper teens—potentially too old to show such severe symptoms. Furthermore, any child who ate bread made from infected grains would have shown symptoms, but only girls were the accusers.

Other objections to this theory include the fact that the "level of ergot poisoning required to present the strong symptoms shown by the afflicted would require amounts of ergot strong enough to affect adults,"[5] yet none of the victims' other family members were affected. In addition, most of the victims showed only one or two symptoms of ergotism and didn't have the long-term health problems that

Shown here is ergot fungus growing on wheat. If the fungus wasn't noticed when the wheat was harvested, it would be ground up with the wheat and eaten in baked goods.

generally go along with it. Also, the affected girls appeared to be able to stop and start their symptoms whenever they wanted, depending on who was watching, which would be impossible if they were caused by a fungus.

The third most common reason given for the illnesses that set off the witch trials was that the girls were simply faking it. Most historians believe that while some of the girls were probably genuinely ill, others copied their symptoms for political or social gain. One girl was caught in a lie in court when she claimed one of the accused, Sarah Good, had stabbed her with a knife, which broke during the attack. She showed the court the broken knife blade and a man who was present at the trial stood up and said he had broken that knife and thrown it away the previous day; clearly the girl had picked up the blade to back up her false story. Furthermore, there's some evidence to suggest that Samuel Parris also lied in court to punish the accused—some of whom had been critical of him in the past. All of this sheds doubt on the rest of the trial and makes it difficult, so many years later, to determine how much of what was said and done during the trials was true.

Unexplained Behaviors

Although the reasons remain unclear, we know that in January 1692, Betty and Abigail started having fits that involved screaming, twitching, fainting, yelling nonsense words, throwing things, and claiming to see things no one else could. They had fevers; they complained of being pinched and poked even when no one was near them; and they behaved oddly, doing things such as running around the room for seemingly no reason. Soon after, Ann Putnam Jr., Mercy Lewis, and Mary Walcott began behaving similarly. Mary Walcott even appeared to have been bitten by some invisible entity.

The parents of the afflicted girls were, quite understandably, disturbed and concerned by these odd behaviors and incidents. Parris at first resorted to fasting and praying. He hoped that these traditional religious rituals would make the strange symptoms go away. When this approach did not work, Parris called on the local doctor, William Griggs. After a thorough examination, Griggs concluded that the devil, a witch, or some other evil being was causing the symptoms.

Meanwhile, the girls' fits became more frequent and dramatic. Puritans were supposed to be quiet during church services, but the girls interrupted the services often. They did more than just have fits too. They sometimes told the person delivering the sermon to sit down, and they would sometimes exclaim that the sermon was too long. These remarks against the church and its leaders were seen as signs of the devil's work. The girls also interrupted church services to claim that they were seeing visions, including a recurring vision of a bird in the church.

Extremely concerned, Mary Sibley—the aunt of Mary Walcott and a neighbor of the Parrises—decided to try using traditional English folk magic to figure out who was bewitching the girls. At the time, folk magic was considered different than witchcraft; it had been practiced for years and was generally considered harmless unless things got out of hand, in which case people who practiced folk magic were often accused of practicing witchcraft as well. Mary Sibley's folk magic involved baking a witch cake by mixing flour or ashes with the girls' urine and feeding it to a dog. There are various beliefs on how the witch cake worked; some said the dog would start acting strangely, while others believed the witch's essence was in the urine and the witch would be harmed when the dog bit into the cake. Either way, Puritans at that time believed the remedy would point out the guilty witch.

Sibley convinced Tituba and her husband to bake the witch cake and feed it to the Parris family's dog. When Parris found out, he was outraged because he saw all magic as a tool of the devil. He pressured Abigail and Betty to name the witch who was tormenting them. It is likely that the pressure grew to be too much for the young

THEY MADE HISTORY: MARY SIBLEY

Mary Sibley was born Mary Woodrow in Salem in 1660. In 1686, she married Samuel Sibley and had seven children with him in the following years. When her niece and young neighbors started showing strange symptoms, she suggested the witch cake as a possible solution. This was done on February 25, 1692, but it didn't have the desired effect. In fact, the same day, two more girls—their friend, 12-year-old Ann Putnam Jr., and 17-year-old Elizabeth Hubbard, the niece of the doctor who had tried to treat Abigail and Betty—began showing the same symptoms, which lends some support to the mass psychogenic illness theory.

Samuel Parris scolded Mary Sibley privately, and he publicly told his congregation that they should never do anything like that again. As a punishment for Sibley, he refused to give her communion—a practice that is important to Christians in their church services—until she confessed in front of the entire church the following month. Nothing after her involvement in the witch cake incident is known for certain about Mary Sibley's life, although it has been suggested that she died around 1760 at the age of 100.

girls to handle, so to make Parris stop bothering them, they named a vulnerable member of the community who was known to dabble in magic: Tituba.

How You See History

1. Do you think anything could have prevented the witch trials from happening? Explain your answer.
2. What do you think is the most convincing explanation or combination of explanations for the girls' fits?
3. Why do you think folk magic was generally tolerated in Puritan society, but witchcraft wasn't?

CHAPTER THREE

ACCUSATIONS AND TRIALS

On February 26, 1692, Abigail and Betty accused Tituba of bewitching them. Several neighbors and ministers were asked to question Tituba and observe the girls' behavior, which had been growing stranger. On February 27, Ann Putnam Jr. and Elizabeth Hubbard accused Sarah Osborne (sometimes written Osborn) and Sarah Good of causing their symptoms. Like Tituba, these women were vulnerable and easy to accuse: Good was a homeless beggar, and Osborne was "involved with conflicts around inheriting property and also had married, to a local scandal, an indentured servant. None of these three were likely to have many local defenders against such accusations."[1]

After the public accusations were made, formal complaints were brought to Salem Town to begin the process of charging the three women. The complaints came from four men of Salem, one of whom was Ann Putnam Jr.'s father. On March 1, the three women were brought in for initial questioning by two magistrates, John Hathorne and Jonathan Corwin. Tituba confessed and said the other two women were also witches, Sarah Osborne said she was innocent, and Sarah Good said she herself was innocent but Tituba and Osborne weren't. In the end, all three women were believed to be guilty, so the magistrates concluded that there was enough evidence and cause to have a proper trial.

Today, visitors to Salem can view Judge Jonathan Corwin's house, which has been renamed the Witch House.

THEY MADE HISTORY: TITUBA

When Tituba was brought in for questioning before the magistrates, she immediately confessed, giving many specific details about what she had done to the girls who were accusing her. She also apologized for her actions, saying she loved Betty and never meant to hurt her. On the surface, this seems like a bizarre thing to do when, as we know now, she was obviously innocent. Since the people of Salem had no reason to suspect she was lying, the reason why she did this was never recorded, but today there are a few theories. One is that her confession was tortured out of her. Parris had questioned her himself immediately after Abigail and Betty accused her, and she had maintained her innocence. It's likely that he beat her in anger when she refused to confess, which could at least partially explain her confession in the second round of questioning.

Another theory—one that could be true whether or not Parris did torture her—is that Tituba realized confessing was the only way she could avoid being killed. As one author pointed out, "Puritans hate liars, but they can't deny a good request for forgiveness."[1] Instead of being killed like many of the women who denied that they were witches, Tituba was imprisoned for 15 months and then sold to another master in April 1693. Nothing more is known about her.

1. Christobel Hastings, "The True Story of Tituba, the Slave at the Center of the Salem Witch Trials," Vice, October 15, 2018, www.vice.com/en_us/article/7x3jbq/the-true-story-of-tituba-the-slave-at-the-center-of-the-salem-witch-trials.

Targeting the Least Powerful

Certainly it is no coincidence that the first people accused of being witches were not wealthy citizens with sterling reputations and connections in high places. Nor is it surprising that at first no men were accused; after all, men were seen as the community's leading citizens and the guardians and enforcers of order and conformity.

Rather, the initial targets were older women whose reputations were already questionable. As women, they were assumed from the start to be weak, easily tricked, cowardly, and more susceptible than men to falling under the control of evil forces. Another black mark against these women was that they were physically unattractive by their society's standards and aging; outward beauty was often taken as a sign of inward goodness, which meant being seen as unattractive was taken as proof of an immoral soul. Still another reason to suspect the women was their outspokenness. People—particularly women—who complained too much, asked too many questions, or said or did things the community considered to be even slightly out of the ordinary were seen as potential agents of sin and evil. The fact that the women were poor and economically and politically powerless also made them easy targets.

Tituba, the first to be accused of practicing witchcraft, conveniently fit all of these criteria. Not only was she a woman, she was foreign-born, had dark skin, and spoke with a noticeable accent. Moreover, Tituba came from a non-Christian society that had, by English and Puritan standards, strange, unwholesome customs, including some associated with magic and evil beings. Considering these attributes, in any witch hunt in a white Christian community, a woman like Tituba was a natural scapegoat.

The second victim of the witch hysteria, Sarah Good, also bore a number of social black marks in addition to her gender that made her a likely suspect. First, she was poor and lived in disgrace on the fringes of the community. Her poverty had been the result of a series of financial disasters during her two marriages, which had left her a beggar. Her disgrace came in part from the suicide of her father, John Solart, in 1672, which was an act condemned by Puritans. Sarah Good's physical appearance also made her a natural suspect in the witch hunt. Though she was only around 40, her hard life had taken a toll, and she looked closer to 70, with a bent back, a wrinkled face, prematurely gray hair, and a raspy voice. In other words, she looked and sounded like the stereotype of a witch.

Sarah Osborne, the third woman the girls accused of being a witch, had also had a difficult life. Her prosperous first husband,

Today, movies and TV shows often show witches as being young and beautiful. However, in the past, the stereotypical witch was old and scary, such as the depiction shown here.

Robert Prince, had died, after which she had married her penniless indentured servant, Alexander Osborne. Later, she had become disabled; by the time she was accused of witchcraft, she was 49, poverty-stricken, and bedridden from illness. Because of her physical illness, Sarah Osborne could not make it to church on Sundays. This was another black mark against her, as Puritan elders expected everyone to attend services, no matter how physically incapacitated they might be.

Questioning the Suspects

Although the questioning was a serious legal procedure, neither of the officials had any formal legal training; there simply were no qualified lawyers in Massachusetts Bay. At this point in American history, Massachusetts was still a colony of England and therefore should have followed British law. However, in her book *The Devil in Massachusetts: A Modern Enquiry into the Salem Witch Trials*, Marion L. Starkey noted that the Puritans "did not permit the professional practice of law in the colony. In effect, the administration of the law was in the hands of laymen, most of them second-generation colonists who had an incomplete grasp of current principles of English jurisdiction."[2]

Under these circumstances, the accused women were at yet another disadvantage: They lacked legal rights and representation. The men in charge of both the questioning sessions and trials had little understanding of the English idea that an accused person is innocent until proven guilty. Instead, they considered the women guilty until proven innocent and believed they didn't have the right to legal representation. They were focused on getting a confession—not finding out the truth.

For several months, the investigation focused on more informal questioning; the trials didn't really start until May. Until then, the accused were brought either to the meetinghouse or a local tavern to be questioned by magistrates. People who were considered to be witches were imprisoned until the trials officially started.

In a modern courtroom, questions must be asked as neutrally as possible. This is why, instead of asking, "Were you at the scene of the crime last night?" a lawyer might ask, "Where were you last night?" Since the Salem magistrates weren't lawyers, they asked accusing questions. Having the subject approached this way made it easy for the accused to accidentally incriminate themselves.

After the first round of questioning, Hathorne asked Betty and the other girls if they were sure that Sarah Good was their tormentor. The girls insisted she was. Furthermore, they said, Good had harassed them that very morning by sending her specter, or invisible evil spirit, to pinch and assault them. Hathorne continued to interrogate Good, asking, "Do you not see now what you have done? Why do you not tell us the truth? Why do you thus torment these poor children?"[3]

During the questioning and the formal trials, the afflicted girls were present and often demonstrated their symptoms for the audience, claiming that the person who was being questioned was hurting them.

Good maintained her innocence, but the magistrates, having already decided she was guilty, decided she must be lying and therefore should be held for trial.

Sarah Osborne was next to be questioned. Hathorne asked her some of the same initial questions he had asked Sarah Good, beginning with what evil spirits she was familiar with. Osborne declared that she had no such familiarity, nor had she ever seen the devil, nor consorted with any of the devil's helpers. Then, Hathorne abruptly changed the direction of the questioning to her familiarity with Sarah Good. He was seeking to incriminate the present suspect by linking her with the other accused woman. Osborne denied having any familiarity with Sarah Good and claimed she had not seen her in two years.

Next, as he had done earlier while questioning Sarah Good, Hathorne addressed himself to the afflicted girls. He asked them to confirm that Sarah Osborne had tormented them, and they replied that she had. At this point, Osborne asserted that she was not only innocent but also more likely to be the victim rather than the perpetrator of witchcraft. When Hathorne asked what she meant, she told him how she had once dreamed that she saw the form of a person with dark skin near her bed. It had pinched her and pulled her hair.

Finally, Hathorne attempted to hurt Osborne's reputation by emphasizing her lack of church attendance. She insisted that poor health had kept her from attending services. However, this did not satisfy Hathorne and Corwin. They decided that she, like Sarah Good, should be held for trial.

The last woman to be questioned that day was Tituba, who admitted her involvement in supernatural affairs. Tituba told Hathorne and Corwin that there were women that would hurt the girls. When asked to name them, she answered Sarah Good, Sarah Osborne, and two other women she claimed not to know, who came to Salem from Boston accompanied by a strange, tall man. In a long round of questioning, Tituba claimed that the four witches had been aided by several evil animals, including a black dog, a yellow bird, and some cats. All the witches and animals had sometimes taken invisible forms.

Suddenly, Betty and Abigail began having convulsions, causing murmurs of astonishment and fear to ripple through the room. Hathorne quickly used this outburst to his advantage, asking

One common myth held that witches could transform themselves into animals—most frequently hares or birds in Western stories. It was also believed that they kept cats as familiars, or pets who helped with their witchcraft, and that witches could send a demon in the form of a dog to bewitch someone. These stories, unfortunately, often caused people to harm animals, especially black cats and dogs.

Tituba, "Do you see who it is who torments these children now?" "Yes," she replied. "It is Goody Good. She hurts them in her own shape."[4]

HISTORY HAPPENED HERE: SALEM, MASSACHUSETTS

Today, Salem is a bustling town with many excellent restaurants, luxurious hotels, and entertaining attractions. In addition to things most American towns have, such as movie theaters and gaming arcades, Salem has dozens of attractions centered on its history with witches, including a 3-D documentary about the witch trials, a museum about the events of 1692, and a memorial to the people who were killed.

In Salem, there are also many psychics, shops for modern-day witches, and a tour of the town that promises to teach visitors the facts about what being a practicing witch means today. None of these have anything to do with the witch trials, but the loose connection to the concept of witchcraft and the modern fascination with magic has created the idea of Salem as a mystical place. Some people find it fun and exciting, while others see it as silly or even disrespectful to the original witch trial victims. Festivities around Halloween include traditional "scary" things such as a wax museum display of Frankenstein's castle as well as "witchy" events, such as a live performance called Moon Witch that ends with a tarot card reading for everyone who attends. All in all, the Salem of today would be completely unrecognizable to the people who lived there in 1692.

Tituba's confession proved pivotal because it did irreparable harm to Sarah Good and Sarah Osborne, as well as to the community. Some historians have even suggested that the trials wouldn't have gone as far as they did if Tituba hadn't confessed; her statement that other witches were loose in the region significantly increased the witch hysteria that already existed in Salem. From that moment on, nearly everyone was on the lookout for evil witches in their midst. However, at the time, it's likely that her focus was on saving her own life; she couldn't have foreseen the effects her confession might have.

More Witches

Sarah Good, Sarah Osborne, and Tituba were put in jail and occasionally questioned again, but that wasn't the end of the event. Other girls started having fits, including Mary Warren and Mercy Lewis, two servants in the homes of prominent citizens.

On March 11, 1692, Ann Putnam Jr. started showing the same symptoms as her friends Betty and Abigail. She claimed that Martha Corey, an upstanding member of the community and a regular churchgoer, was tormenting her. Thomas Putnam and some other men went to Corey's house on March 12 and questioned her informally. On March 20, Abigail interrupted church to say that she saw Martha's spirit leave her body, so on March 21, Martha was arrested and formally questioned. According to a later report by the Reverend Deodat Lawson, three of the supposedly bewitched girls "vehemently accused [Corey] in the assembly of afflicting them, by biting, pinching, strangling, etc. and that they did in their fit see her likeness coming to them."[5] In spite of—or perhaps because of—Corey's repeated protestations of innocence, the magistrates were satisfied that she must be a witch and ordered her thrown into jail to await trial.

As *Encyclopedia Britannica* pointed out, "Those who confessed—or confessed and named other witches—were spared the court's vengeance, owing to the Puritan belief that they would receive their punishment from God."[6] This was part of the reason why the witch trials continued as long as they did: Confessing was a sure way for an accused woman to save herself from execution, but doing so fanned the flames by making it look like the accusers were telling the truth and prompting the town to keep looking for witches.

From then on, the accusations started to come faster, and the people targeted went from eccentrics and outcasts to people the accusers might have had problems with. On March 19, Abigail Williams claimed that the specter of another respectable churchgoer, Rebecca Nurse, was tormenting her, so on March 24, the 71-year-old woman was arrested and questioned. Around the same time, Dorcas Good, Sarah Good's four-year-old daughter, was arrested and questioned. The defenseless child, who had no real idea of what was happening, said something that was interpreted as a confession that both she and her mother had practiced witchcraft, so she ended up in prison with the other accused witches.

Speaking Out

Some residents of Salem, especially those whose family members had been accused, felt that the witch hunt had gone too far. However, any

This illustration from 1880 shows Martha Corey (*right*) protesting her imprisonment.

FROM THE SOURCE: THE DEPOSITION OF MARY DANIEL

Although it originally started in Salem Village, the 1692 witch hunt eventually spread outward to other parts of Massachusetts. Some documents have survived better than others, so some of the accusers such as Betty Parris and accused such as Rebecca Nurse are far better known than others. One lesser-known trial involved charges of witchcraft brought against 77-year-old widow Margaret Scott of Rawley, Massachusetts, by 19-year-old Mary Daniel. Daniel's deposition, or accusation, reads in part:

> *I ... felt a great pricking in ye soles of my feet, and after a while I saw apparently the shape of Margret Scott, who, as I was sitting in a chair by ye fire pulled me with ye chair, down backward to ye ground, and tormented and pinched me very much, and I saw her go away at ye door, in which fit I was dumb [silent] and so continued till ye next morning, finding a great load and heaviness upon my tongue.*[1]

Because of this deposition and other accusations against Scott, the widow was hanged on September 22, 1692, with seven other accused witches.

1. Quoted in Sarah Pruitt, "Read the Document That Condemned a Woman to Death in the Salem Witch Trials," History.com, modified August 30, 2018, www.history.com/news/read-the-document-that-condemned-a-woman-to-death-in-the-salem-witch-trials.

dissent came with a heavy price, as the circle of accusations widened to include them too. Farmer John Proctor's servant, Mary Warren, was among the girls having fits, and it had already been suggested by some of the girls that his wife, Elizabeth Proctor, might be a witch. Furthermore, his daughter was related to

Rebecca Nurse through marriage. From the start, John Proctor had repeatedly voiced his objections to the witch trials and had also publicly denounced the girls, accusing them of faking the whole thing and maintaining that Elizabeth and Rebecca were innocent. By some accounts, he also either threatened to beat or did beat Mary Warren as punishment for faking her fits. As a result, John Proctor himself was accused of witchcraft and arrested.

Similarly, when Sarah Cloyce defended her sister, Rebecca Nurse, she was also accused and arrested. The circle of accusations and arrests was widening at an alarming rate and there seemed no end in sight. It's likely that even some of the afflicted girls thought things had gotten out of control, but by this point, so many accusations had been made that they didn't know how they could go back; the understanding of the magnitude of punishment linked with that kind of lie was too much to bear. Similarly, the elders who stood with the young girls did not want their credibility to be ruined, which in turn would ruin their reputation. The answer was to continue the trials, each person going into them with a personal mission to not come out as a liar. This fact alone caused the intense persistence that led to the loss of so many lives.

In April, more than 50 men in Salem Village and the surrounding towns signed petitions declaring that they didn't believe John and Elizabeth Proctor were witches. A few days after John Proctor's arrest on April 11, Mary Warren said she had lied about him, but on April 19, she took her statement back. On April 16, in fear that they would be seen as liars, the other girls turned on Warren, stating that she had begun working with the devil and practicing witchcraft. After an intensive session of questioning, Warren retracted her previous statement of no longer being afflicted. This implies that Mary Warren realized her only chance of survival was to continue lying. The girls continued accusing people, and sometimes the accused, in turn, accused others, leading to more and more arrests. In all, by the time the witch trials ended, 200 people had been accused of witchcraft—and it's worth noting that "many of the accused proved to be enemies of the Putnams, and Putnam

This 1899 illustration of the 1692 witch trials shows an accused woman begging the court for mercy. Everyone who was accused of witchcraft was innocent, but standing up for the accused could have dangerous consequences.

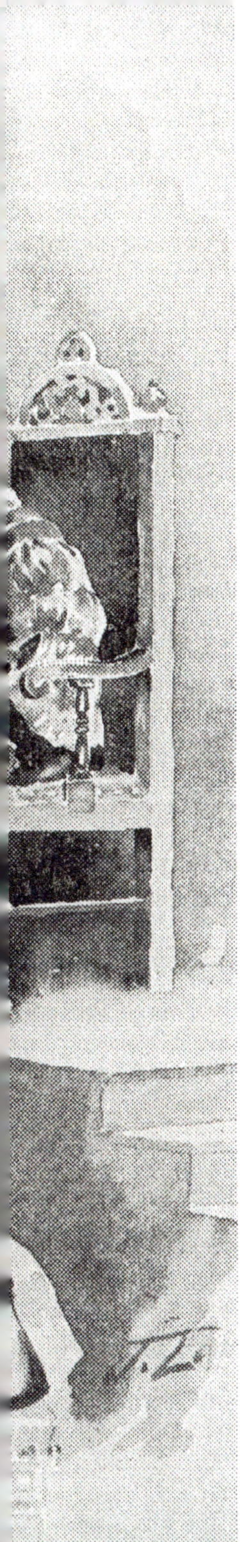

family members and in-laws would end up being the accusers in dozens of cases."[7]

Going to Trial

The trials could not begin until the Massachusetts Bay Colony had a new charter from England. The colony's original charter had lapsed three years before, leaving its inhabitants in a sort of legal limbo in which no legally sanctioned trials could be conducted. To remedy this situation, the widely respected minister Increase Mather had recently journeyed to England to petition the government for a new colonial charter. He returned in the middle of May 1692 with the charter in hand, which meant that the trials could begin shortly afterward.

Mather brought with him a new colonial governor, Sir William Phips, whose authority was needed to set up the court and appoint its judges. Phips arrived to see the local jails overflowing and realized that he had his work cut out for him. He set up a court of "Oyer and Terminer," an old Anglo-French legal phrase that meant "to hear and determine." It referred to a special court convened to hear criminal cases. Phips authorized the creation of the court on May 27 and selected seven judges. The head of the court was Massachusetts lieutenant governor William Stoughton, who lived in Dorchester. The others were Bostonians John Richards, Peter Sergeant, Samuel Sewall, and Waitstill Winthrop, along with Nathaniel Saltonstall from Haverhill and Bartholomew Gedney from Salem.

In the 1690s, based on precedent in earlier cases in the colony and in England, several kinds of evidence were allowed to be presented in court that today would be viewed as highly prejudiced or illogical. For example, one kind of evidence that supposedly proved someone was an agent of the devil was their inability to recite the Lord's Prayer without error. Aside from not being evidence of any kind, this test didn't take into account that

A specter is a person's ghostly form, similar to the image shown here. The admission of spectral evidence in court allowed accusers to say they had seen the specter of an accused person, which made it easier to convict innocent people.

someone might make mistakes simply because they were nervous. Also, if someone who had confessed to being a witch proceeded to accuse someone else, it was seen as acceptable evidence. Furthermore, spectral evidence—claims made by various persons that they had witnessed specters harassing people—was also permissible in court when the trials started. The reason for this was, the judges said, witches couldn't take on the image of an innocent person. Therefore, if someone claimed to have seen the image of an accused person in their house or somewhere else they couldn't possibly physically be at the time, it was clear proof that they were witches. The idea that someone might be lying about seeing a spectral form didn't seem to occur to them, even though not everyone could see these specters.

Other kinds of acceptable evidence in witchcraft cases involved the discovery of physical proof on the bodies of the accused. If any mark was found on their skin—which was a frequent occurrence, since scars and birthmarks counted—a pin test was performed, in which the examiner pierced the mark with a pin. If it didn't bleed, it was viewed as another sign of the devil's work. In some cases, examiners used fraud to make sure someone was convicted: They used a dull pin that wouldn't break the skin. In the case of another kind of evidence—the touch test—the accused was forced to touch someone who was having a witchcraft-induced fit. If the fit suddenly stopped, it supposedly proved that the specter afflicting the victim had jumped back into the body of the accused, and therefore the accused was guilty.

PAST MEETS PRESENT: CRY INNOCENT

Cry Innocent is an immersive theater production that allows people to play the role of the jury in Bridget Bishop's trial in 1692. It begins with an outdoor scene in which Bishop is arrested and continues indoors for about 45 minutes. During this time, the audience is encouraged to ask questions, examine the evidence, and vote on Bishop's guilt or innocence. The goal of the performance is to help people understand the way the Puritans were thinking during the trials and give a more complex picture of why the events happened the way they did. As Kristina Stevick, the project's artistic director, explained, "What I would hope is that a person who has had 45 minutes to flirt with a 17th-century English mindset ... would understand why a person *might* accuse somebody of witchcraft."[1]

1. Quoted in Tara Isabella Burton, "There Weren't Any Witches in Salem in 1693. But There Sure Are Now," Vox, October 30, 2017, www.vox.com/identities/2017/10/30/16560092/salem-witch-trials-magic-halloween-witchcraft-arthur-miller-crucible-past.

Even if someone passed all these tests, they might not be set free. In one example, Reverend George Burroughs recited the Lord's Prayer without any mistakes right before his scheduled execution. According to History.com, "The performance was dismissed as a devil's trick, and the hanging proceeded as planned."[8]

As accusations and arrests continued, the Court of Oyer and Terminer held its first trial on June 8, 1692, to decide the fate of Bridget Bishop, a middle-aged tavern keeper. Although it's not known for certain why she was accused, historians have a few theories. One is that her second husband's children accused her because they wanted the property she'd inherited. Another was that, like the first three women who were accused, she was an easy target:

> *her behavior was often disagreeable in a community that valued harmony and obedience to authority … she violated community norms by having associated with the wrong people, keeping "unreasonable" hours, hosting drinking and gambling parties, and behaving immorally. She was known for publicly fighting with her husbands (she was in her third marriage when accused in 1692). She was known for wearing a scarlet bodice, considered a bit less "Puritan" than was acceptable to some in the community.*[9]

In addition to all of this, Bishop had been accused of witchcraft about 12 years before, though she had never been legally tried.

A number of Bishop's neighbors and acquaintances recounted strange events that happened when she was around. However, the court was most swayed by the so-called evidence found by workmen who had helped renovate a house Bishop had lived in a few years before. They claimed that, inside the walls, they had found poppets, which are small, human-like figures used to do harm to a particular person. It is generally believed that a poppet can be tied to a real person by adding a piece of that person's body, such as hair, to the doll. A voodoo doll is one example of a poppet.

When asked about the poppets hidden in the wall, Bridget Bishop claimed she had no idea how they got there. However, the judges and men making up the jury did not believe her, partly because they already assumed she must be guilty. As in all the cases heard in the Salem witch trials, the initial questionings determined the suspects' guilt. The court trials constituted little more than legal confirmation of guilt. Thus, no one was surprised

Shown here is an illustration of Bridget Bishop's execution.

when the court found Bishop guilty of being a witch and sentenced her to be executed. On June 10, 1692, only eight days after her trial, Bridget Bishop was hanged—the first death of the Salem witch trials.

How You See History

1. What would you do if you were accused during the witch trials? What would you do if your friend was accused?
2. What legends have you heard about witches? Do we still talk about them the same way today?
3. Why were the witch tests unfair?

CHAPTER FOUR

INNOCENT PEOPLE KILLED

The trial and execution of Bridget Bishop sent shock waves through the Puritan communities of Massachusetts. Certainly the other accused witches in jail now despaired more than ever for their own lives. If Bishop had been found guilty and hanged so quickly, would they suffer similarly? A few people in high places were disturbed for different reasons. One of the judges, Nathaniel Saltonstall, thought the evidence against Bishop had been flimsy. Moreover, he felt that the cruel way she was treated on the day of her execution was un-Christian and reprehensible, so he resigned from the court. Jonathan Corwin, who had helped run the pretrial questioning sessions, took his place. In addition, a group of local ministers voiced their concerns about the admission of spectral evidence in the trials. Like Saltonstall, they worried that it was unreliable. In fact, on June 15, Cotton Mather, a Bostonian minister and the son of Increase Mather, wrote a letter to the Court of Oyer and Terminer urging them not to rely on spectral evidence. However, the remaining judges disagreed, and such evidence remained admissible.

Initial Misgivings

The witch trials resumed on June 29. On that day and the next, five women were tried. One of them was Sarah Good, who had been held in jail since her initial questioning in March. Tituba

◀ Accused witches were held in jail cells similar to the one shown here.

had confessed, so there was no need for a trial, and Sarah Osborne, who had already been in poor health, died in jail shortly after she was imprisoned. The other women who were tried with Sarah Good were Sarah Wildes, Elizabeth Howe, Susannah Martin, and Rebecca Nurse. As had happened during the earlier questioning sessions, Betty Parris, Abigail Williams, and the other supposedly afflicted girls were allowed to be present. The girls repeatedly threw fits and claimed that the defendants' specters were tormenting them.

In the eyes of those present, the most remarkable of the five cases tried at the end of June 1692 was that of Rebecca Nurse, who was considered an upstanding citizen and one of the least likely people to be a witch. Thirty-nine local residents mustered the nerve to sign a petition on her behalf that stated they believed her to be completely innocent. One of them was the influential John Putnam, brother of Thomas Putnam, who had earlier denounced Nurse but then changed his mind. The members of the jury found themselves agreeing with the petitioners, as Nurse presented herself in court as a respectable Christian woman. Thus, the jury initially found her innocent.

However, immediately after the verdict was announced, the afflicted girls went into violent spasms. At the same time, hundreds of onlookers, including those who had earlier denounced and questioned the defendants, voiced their outrage with the decision.

Seeing all this commotion, the judges asked the jurors to reconsider. They reviewed the testimony and found that she had failed to answer one of the questions. A juror had asked her a question about her statement that a woman named Deliverance Hobbs was "one of us." However, because Nurse was partially deaf as well as elderly, ill, and distraught, she did not hear it and remained silent. To the jury, this was a good enough excuse to change Nurse's verdict to guilty. Only later was she told that she had been asked the question and had failed to answer it, thereby sealing her fate. She therefore wrote an appeal to the court, explaining that she had simply not heard the question. Nurse also explained that her statement about Hobbs reflected their shared status as prisoners, not as witches. Governor Phips granted her a reprieve, but another public outcry caused him to recall it, and Nurse was hanged on July 19 along with Good, Wildes, Howe, and Martin.

At this point, the situation was starting to look grim for the rest of the prisoners. John Proctor wrote a letter from his jail cell to church leaders in Boston, since it was common knowledge that they weren't entirely comfortable with the witch trials taking place in Salem. In his letter, Proctor asked them to either appoint new judges or move the trials to Boston. He knew that if someone as outwardly blameless as Rebecca Nurse could be executed for witchcraft, there was no hope for anyone else. "Nothing but our innocent blood will serve" those who had accused him and his cellmates of witchcraft, he wrote. The judges had "condemned us already before our trials," Proctor complained. Therefore, he and his fellow inmates "beg and implore your favorable assistance of this our humble petition … that if it be possible our innocent blood may be spared."[1]

In the same letter, Proctor exposed another unfair and brutal tactic used by the authorities in their eagerness to root out and destroy suspected witches. He pointed out that much of the so-called evidence against him and the others had been provided by five other suspected witches who had given said evidence under duress. In particular, at least two of these individuals had been tortured. They "would not confess anything," Proctor said, "till they tied them neck and heels till the blood was ready to come out of their noses."[2] The "neck and heels" torture consisted of looping a rope around a person's neck and then tying it to their ankles; this caused extreme discomfort, pain, and often nosebleeds.

A Plea for Rationality

Upon receiving Proctor's letter, the clergy held a meeting on August 1. What they talked about is unknown, but when the meeting was over, they announced that spectral evidence wasn't actually proof of guilt: The devil could, indeed, take the form of an innocent person. However, this announcement wasn't enough to save John Proctor.

When the Proctors went to trial on August 2, 1692, the proceedings went swiftly and, in essence, did no more than confirm the findings of the Proctors' questioning session on April 11. As in all the hearings and trials, much of the testimony and evidence against the defendants had come from the afflicted girls, who were present in the room at all the trials. They claimed that they could see John Proctor's specter in various places around the room and that it was hurting them. Tituba's husband, John Indian, was also one of the accusers.

Although the judges had begun to be suspicious of spectral evidence, John Proctor's real-life actions didn't make him look good. According to the records we have about the trials and the events surrounding them, Proctor frequently threatened or carried out violence. He had been vocally against the trials from the beginning, claiming that all the girls who were accusing people were lying and suggesting that they be whipped or even hanged. Furthermore, the Proctors were social rivals of the Putnams. All of this gave some members of the original group of afflicted girls a motive for singling him out. He had also either beaten or threatened to beat his servant, Mary Warren, as well as John Indian, giving them both a very strong motive to see Proctor sent to jail or executed.

In addition to John and Elizabeth, other members of the Proctor family were accused,

This wall, called Proctor's Ledge Memorial, was unveiled on July 19, 2017, in Salem to commemorate the women who were killed on that date in 1692. Shown here is one of Rebecca Nurse's descendants kneeling in front of Nurse's name on the wall.

REBECCA
NURSE
JULY 19, 1692

often by members or allies of the Putnam family. For example, Elizabeth's sister, Mary Basset DeRich, and sister-in-law, Sarah Basset, were accused by John and Thomas Putnam on behalf of Mary Walcott, Abigail Williams, Mercy Lewis, and Ann Putnam Jr. The Proctors' sons, Benjamin and William, were also accused by or on behalf of several of the other girls. Deciding that there wasn't enough evidence against them, the jury chose not to indict, or formally charge, these accused people. However, the pattern of accusations lends support to the idea that at least some of the accusations were motivated by a desire for some kind of vengeance.

Unsurprisingly, at the end of John and Elizabeth Proctor's trial, they were pronounced guilty and sentenced to death. However, Elizabeth Proctor was pregnant at the time, so she was given a temporary reprieve until her baby was born, after which she was to be hanged. However, for unknown reasons, she was never executed. She gave birth in jail, and she stayed there until May 1693, when anyone who was still imprisoned as a result of being accused of witchcraft was freed by Governor Phips. No one knows if her child survived. John Proctor went to his death on August 19. Either shortly before or after his untimely demise, the local authorities seized all his property and belongings to pay the fees for imprisoning him and his wife. One of the magistrates seized his cattle, sold some at half their market value, and slaughtered the rest for sale to the West Indies. The Proctors' house and barn were stripped of everything, even storage barrels and pots and pans. When she was released from jail, Elizabeth Proctor found she had lost everything.

More Executions

The Proctors were not the only people tried in early August 1692. Martha Carrier, a resident of the town of Andover; John Willard, who spoke out against the witch trials; and George Jacobs Sr., a 72-year-old grandfather who needed two canes to walk, also faced the judges and jury. Much of the evidence against Carrier was provided by neighbors who had had property disputes with her. For instance, a couple named Benjamin and Sarah Abbot claimed they had argued with Martha Carrier about the proper placement of a

THEY MADE HISTORY: ANN FOSTER

Ann Foster was born in England and came to the American colonies in 1635. She and her husband, Andrew Foster, had five children together in Andover, Massachusetts. When another Andover resident named Elizabeth Ballard got sick in 1692 and the doctors couldn't figure out why, they asked Ann Putnam Jr. and Mary Wolcott to come to Andover to see if they could figure out who was bewitching Ballard. When they saw Ann Foster, who was a 70-year-old widow at the time and therefore may have been seen as an easy target, the girls fell into fits.

At first, Foster claimed she was innocent. Then, Ballard's husband Joseph accused Foster's daughter, Mary Lacey Sr., and granddaughter, Mary Lacey Jr. Mary Lacey Jr. accused her mother, who in turn accused her own mother. At that point, Ann Foster confessed, likely to save her daughter. Foster and Lacey Sr. also accused Martha Carrier; she was already in jail awaiting trial, so this may have been an attempt to save themselves while avoiding naming anyone new. Although neither Foster nor her family members were hanged, she and Lacey Sr. were kept in prison even after the trials formally ended. Foster died in prison in December 1692.

boundary running between their two farms and that Carrier had lost her temper and threatened to get back at Benjamin. In his testimony, Benjamin Abbot listed the afflictions supposedly caused by Carrier in her efforts to seek revenge:

> *Presently after [the dispute] I was taken with a swelling in mÿ foott & then was taken with a paÿne in mÿ side … wich bred to a sore: which was lancit [lanced] bÿ doctor prescott … & putt me to verÿ great misserÿ, so that it brought me almost to Deaths doore, & Continued, until goodwiffe [Goodwife] Carrier was Taken … by the Constable & that verÿ daÿ I begun to grow better … & so*

have been well Ever since: & have great cause to think that the [Goodwife] Carrier had a great hand in my sickness & misery.[3]

In addition to supposed evidence of this nature, Martha Carrier was condemned on the accusations of several people who confirmed that she was a witch. These included her own sons, who were severely tortured in jail to force them to denounce their mother, and Ann Foster, a previously accused witch who had confessed and named Carrier as a fellow witch the previous month. Amid the presentation of all this trumped-up evidence, Carrier remained defiant, calling the witnesses and afflicted girls liars and the whole proceedings shameful. This annoyed and, in some cases, enraged the community's authority figures, making them more determined to find her guilty.

As for George Jacobs, one of the afflicted girls named Sarah Churchill and a local boy, John DeRich, claimed that the old man's specter had chased or beaten them. Jacobs realized that he had no way of proving that his specter hadn't done this and seemed resigned to his fate. He is credited with telling the magistrates, "Well, burn me or hang me. I will stand in the truth of [Jesus] Christ!"[4] The judges obliged him by sentencing him to death. Jacobs and Carrier were both hanged on August 19 along with John Proctor. Afterward, the authorities went to Jacobs's home and confiscated everything, including his wife's wedding ring.

Another person who lost his life on August 19 was the Reverend George Burroughs, a former minister in Salem Village who was accused by the Salem girls. He was arrested in Maine, which at that time was a northern province of Massachusetts, and taken to Salem to stand trial. Because he was an unusually muscular and strong man, witnesses claimed that his strength was beyond a normal human's and must have come from the devil. Some people in town believed he was the man Tituba had mentioned seeing with the four women in her testimony.

During the trial, which lasted only a couple of hours at best, Burroughs seemed lost in thought. Perhaps he was in a state of shock over being accused of such crimes when he knew full well that he was innocent. Whatever the reason for Burroughs's silence on the stand, it made him seem all the more guilty to the judges, jury, and onlookers. Despite a petition to set him free signed by 35 Salem citizens, Burroughs was found guilty and sentenced to death.

FROM THE SOURCE: TESTIMONY AGAINST GEORGE BURROUGHS

Ann Putnam Jr. gave a deposition against George Burroughs that stated in part:

> *On the 20th of April, 1692, at evening [I] saw the apparition [specter] of a minister at which [I] was grievously affrighted and cried out … [I asked] "Whence came you, and what is your name, for I will complain of you … if you be a wizard." And immediately I was tortured by him, being racked [stretched] and almost choked by him, and he tempted me to write in his [evil devil's] book, which I refused with loud outcries … Then presently he told me that his name was George Burroughs and that he had had three wives and that he had bewitched the first two of them to death.*[1]

1. Quoted in Frances Hill, ed., *The Salem Witch Trials Reader* (New York, NY: Da Capo, 2000), pp. 194–95.

Death by Pressing

Of the 20 people who were executed in the witch trials—a number that doesn't take into account all the people who died in prison awaiting either their trial or their release—19 were hanged. In September, Giles Corey, a farmer in his 80s, suffered a different kind of death. Corey had testified against his own wife, Martha, in March, in large part because he was caught up in the frenzy of the witch trials and believed the accusations against her that started when

she spoke out against the trials. He told the court that he suspected Martha had made their ox and pet cat sick, and he noted that sometimes his wife would kneel in front of the fireplace as if she were praying, but he never heard her say anything. Later, in April, several of the afflicted girls accused the old man himself, saying that his specter had tormented them. When questioned, Corey had insisted that he was innocent and recanted his testimony about Martha.

At first, Corey had been convinced by the afflicted girls and had willingly participated in the witch trials but changed his mind when he was the one accused. He pled not guilty when he was charged in September, but that was the last time he participated in the proceedings. Not only did he refuse to

Despite perfectly reciting the Lord's Prayer right before his execution—which should have proven he wasn't a witch—George Burroughs was hanged and Cotton Mather reminded the crowd that Burroughs's fate had already been decided by the court.

accuse anyone else of witchcraft or protest his own innocence, he used a legal tactic called "standing mute" when he was asked to accept a trial by a jury of his peers. According to many historians, this may be because he wanted to make sure the court wouldn't seize his estate, as it would have if he had gone to trial and been found guilty.

PAST MEETS PRESENT: THE CRUCIBLE

In 1952, Arthur Miller wrote a play called *The Crucible* that portrayed the events of the Salem witch trials. However, he wrote it in response to Senator Joseph McCarthy's communist hunt, which has also been called the Red Scare. Miller was trying to draw a comparison between the frenzy of the witch trials and the harm done to innocent people who were accused of being communists.

Miller did some research for his play, but he freely admitted that it wasn't historically accurate. The names of the characters are correct, but to keep the play interesting to watch, he made up many details that he couldn't have known or that are contradicted by the historical record. For example, in *The Crucible,* Abigail Williams accuses John and Elizabeth Proctor of witchcraft because she and John had an affair when Abigail worked as a maid in the Proctors' home. When John rejects Abigail, she starts having fits. However, Abigail was never a maid for the Proctors and there's no evidence to suggest any kind of affair between her and John. Other inaccuracies include only two judges rather than the panel of 11 that existed in real life and a scene in which Samuel Parris finds Tituba leading an occult dance in the woods. While *The Crucible* is interesting to watch and is historically important due to its part in the Red Scare, it gets the Salem witch trials very wrong and shouldn't be used as a source of information about them.

The authorities had very seldom encountered such stubbornness by someone accused of a crime. English law at the time said that anyone who stood mute must be submitted to a torture called *peine forte et dure* (French for "a punishment hard and severe"), which was an old European method of obtaining confessions. It was also called "pressing" because it consisted of making the victim lie face-up on the ground, placing a board on their chest, and then loading large rocks onto the board to make it difficult for them to breathe.

When Corey refused to speak, the authorities took him to a field near the courthouse and began pressing him while a crowd of onlookers watched. They hoped that, at some point, the pressing would convince him to give in and cooperate. Instead, he "urged the executioners to increase the weight which was crushing him … [and] told them it was of no use to expect him to yield."[5] After two days, the torture killed him.

Corey's case marked the only instance in the history of the Massachusetts Bay Colony in which pressing was used. However, that didn't make his surviving relatives feel any better. In fact, the entire incident had a sort of unsettling effect on much of the populace. Like Burroughs's recital of the Lord's Prayer before his execution, the cruel killing of Giles Corey made many Puritans wonder if justice was truly being served in the ongoing witch hunt and trials.

How You See History

1. Why do you think the court relied so strongly on spectral evidence?
2. Why did Giles Corey's death seem worse to the residents of Salem than the hanging of the other victims?
3. Do you think the historical inaccuracies in *The Crucible* were necessary? Why or why not?

CHAPTER FIVE

THE END OF THE PANIC

After Giles Corey's death on September 19, 1692, support for the witch trials dropped dramatically. No new accusations were investigated, and only one more mass hanging was carried out: On September 22, Martha Corey and seven others were hanged. Near the end of September, the Court of Oyer and Terminer stopped meeting but didn't disband yet. Support for the admission of spectral evidence was decreasing as well; although it had been brought up before, influential people—including Reverend Increase Mather—started denouncing its use by the court, saying it wasn't reliable evidence.

Shutting It Down

Although support was waning, the girls kept accusing people, even after the September 22 hangings. These accusations increased both in number and outrageousness. The number of those accused by Abigail Williams alone rose to about 57. Meanwhile, rumors were flying: An accused witch claimed she had attended a meeting involving 25 witches, and someone else said that there were more than 300 witches in the colony.

Shown here is Gallows Hill, where it was believed that most of the people who were accused of witchcraft were executed. In January 2016, the Gallows Hill Project determined that, in reality, the hangings took place at the site known as Proctor's Ledge.

FROM THE SOURCE: THOMAS BRATTLE'S PAMPHLET

Some people were outspokenly against the witch trials from the beginning, and Thomas Brattle was one of the more influential protestors. In 1692, he wrote and circulated a pamphlet giving his account of the witch hunt, which he called a delusion, since he didn't believe witchcraft existed. He wrote:

> *[I]n the opinion of many unprejudiced, considerate, and considerable spectators, some of the condemned went out of the world not only with as great protestations, but also with as good shows of innocency, as men could do. They protested their innocency as in the presence of the great God ... They wished ... that their blood might be the last innocent blood shed upon that account. With great affection [emotion], they entreated Mr. Cotton Mather to pray with them. They prayed that God would discover what witchcrafts were among us; they forgave their accusers ... they prayed earnestly for pardon for all other sins ... and [they] seemed to be very sincere, upright, and sensible of their circumstances.*
>
> *Many of these afflicted persons, who have scores of strange fits in a day, yet in the intervals of time [in between] are hale and hearty ... as though nothing had afflicted them ... Furthermore, these afflicted persons do say ... that they can see specters when their eyes are shut ... I am sure they lie, [or] at least speak falsely ... for [this] is an utter impossibility. It is true they may strongly fancy or have things represented in their imaginations when their eyes are shut, and I think this is all that ought to be allowed to these blind, nonsensical girls.*[1]

With support for the witch trials decreasing anyway after Corey's death, it wasn't hard for Brattle to convince people to give up the hunt.

1. Quoted in Frances Hill, ed., *The Salem Witch Trials Reader* (New York, NY: Da Capo, 2000), p. 98.

By October 1, 1692, about 150 accused witches were sitting in colonial jails, and many more had been accused of witchcraft but were not yet arrested because there was no more room in those jails.

It was not simply the numbers of suspected witches that had begun to strain believability; it was also who was being accused. Throughout most of the witch hunt, hearings, and trials, the vast majority of suspects had been poor, or at least of modest means. Furthermore, although some were considered upstanding members of society, they were generally politically powerless. However, in late September and early October, the afflicted girls began accusing people of much higher standing in the community. The mother-in-law of magistrate Jonathan Corwin was accused of being a witch, for instance. Also accused were the two sons of a well-respected former governor, Simon Bradstreet, and the wife of the Reverend John Hale, one of the most distinguished church leaders in New England. Finally, Lady Mary Phips, wife of governor William Phips, was publicly accused of practicing witchcraft. It is revealing that none of these people were arrested, nor were the accusations against them taken seriously, even for a moment. Clearly, the supposedly afflicted girls had finally gone too far.

Historians have pointed out that the accusers had made two fundamental mistakes. First, there were simply too many witches. It was one thing to accuse a few members of society of being evil agents of the devil; it was quite another to claim that the colony was riddled with hundreds or thousands of witches. Even the most gullible and religiously devout members of the community began to see that such claims had to be excessive and therefore that the accusers themselves could not be trusted.

Second, in their youthful ignorance, the girls eventually thought they could bring down the rich and powerful people who ran their society. However, this was self-delusion. As has been true time after time in history, those in power could not be easily dislodged from their high positions.

PAST MEETS PRESENT: THE LEGEND OF GILES COREY

Although the Salem witch trials have long been over, some people believe their effects can still be felt. Local legend says that Giles Corey's ghost still haunts Salem and can be seen before or after something terrible happens to the town. In one example, people reported seeing the specter of an old man floating through the Howard Street Cemetery in 1914, right before a fire destroyed much of the town.

Some people also believe that Corey cursed the sheriffs of Salem for decades:

> *It has long been rumored that Corey placed a curse on Salem and its sheriff during his torture by shouting …* "I curse you and Salem!" *at the sheriff before he died. Four years after Corey's death, Sheriff [George] Corwin died suddenly of a heart attack at just 30 years old. Local legend suggests that Corey not only cursed Corwin but every Salem sheriff since 1692.*
>
> *In the 1970s, after Salem Sheriff Robert E. Cahill was forced to retire early due to a stroke, heart attack and rare blood condition, he looked into the history of the sheriff's office … The previous sheriff had suffered heart problems as well. "So have all the others, as far back as I could trace," he says. "And the two men who have followed me have had an awful lot of [legal] trouble." Cahill believes that when the sheriff's office was moved from Salem to the new prison in Middleton in 1991, it broke the curse and spared future sheriffs. Since the move, no sheriffs have been diagnosed with any heart conditions or blood ailments.*[1]

1. Rebecca Beatrice Brooks, "The Curse of Giles Corey," *History of Massachusetts* (blog), October 12, 2011, historyofmassachusetts.org/the-curse-of-giles-corey.

An End in Sight

Throughout October, the witch trials were slowly winding down. On October 3, Increase Mather denounced the court's use of spectral evidence more harshly than his son, Cotton Mather, had done earlier in the year. On October 8, influenced by Mather and other prominent ministers from Boston, Governor Phips ordered the court to stop allowing spectral evidence at all and wrote to officials in England, letting them know he had stopped the witch trials. However, this wasn't entirely true yet; although there were no more trials and some of the prisoners were released if they or their families could afford to pay their bail, it wasn't until October 29—when his own wife was accused—that Phips ordered officials to stop arresting people. He disbanded the Court of Oyer and Terminer.

However, though the witchcraft trials had ended, the local jails were still full of people who had been accused of evil doings. The dilemma the governor and other community leaders now faced was what to do with these prisoners. At first, the officials were reluctant to simply release them all. After all, what if some of them were indeed witches? The fact that the afflicted girls had gone too far by accusing Lady Phips of being a witch didn't necessarily indicate that all of the earlier accusations had been wrong.

The solution seemed to be to create a new court called the Superior Court of Judicature, which Phips did on November 25. Its mandate would be not to try new witches but to decide which of the prisoners could safely be released and which should remain in custody. The expectation was that the new court would be much fairer than the earlier one because no spectral evidence would be allowed. Indeed, without the girls' testimony that they saw invisible beings harassing them and others, little other convincing evidence of witchcraft remained. When the new court tried 56 of the prisoners in January 1693, 53 had their cases speedily dismissed. The other three people were found guilty, mainly because they had confessed to being witches.

THEY MADE HISTORY: GOVERNOR WILLIAM PHIPS

William Phips was born in Maine on February 2, 1651, to a moderately wealthy family. Instead of going to school, he was apprenticed to a ship carpenter and later became one himself. He moved to Boston, married Mary Spencer Hull in 1673, and used his improved social influence to become a ship captain. He spent his time at sea looking for sunken treasure, eventually recovering more than 210,000 British pounds' worth—equivalent to more than $49 million in today's American dollars. Part of this was given to the British government, but Phips was allowed to keep 11,000 pounds, or more than $2 million.

In 1689, Phips further increased his social standing by befriending Cotton and Increase Mather, who used their influence to make sure Phips received the post of Royal Governor of Massachusetts despite his lack of experience. Because he held this position, he was able to legally create the Court of Oyer and Terminer and appoint judges to it. However, due to his lack of experience in legal matters and his desire to please influential members of colonial society, he appointed William Stoughton head of the court—a huge mistake, as Stoughton "was a biased judge who believed strongly in witchcraft and the accusations of the girls."[1] According to the Salem Witch Trials Documentary Archive and Transcription Project by the University of Virginia, "Though Phips did eventually put an end to the Court, his failure to control the court's aggressive actions during the summer allowed the persecutions to continue."[2] Although history credits him with ending the witch trials, it's worth remembering that if not for him and the position he was given solely as a result of his wealth and social influence, they would never have happened in the first place.

1. Grace A., "Corruption in the Colony: The Story of Governor William Phips," University of Chicago, accessed September 18, 2019, people.ucls.uchicago.edu/~snekros/New%20World%20News/New_World_News/Corruption_in_the_Colony.html.

2. Brendan Digan, "Governor, Sir William Phips," Salem Witch Trials Documentary Archive and Transcription Project, Spring 2001, salem.lib.virginia.edu/people/phips.html.

Governor William Phips's incompetence and desire to please people who had helped him increase his social standing were major causes of the witch trials.

Though by law the three convicted people were subject to the death penalty, they were never executed. Governor Phips granted them pardons, saying, "Considering how the matter had been managed I sent a reprieve whereby the execucion was stopped." Furthermore, Phips stated that he wanted to eliminate

> *the blak cloud that threatened this Province with destruction; for … this delusion of the Devill did spread and its dismall effects touched the lives and estates of many of their Ma'ties [Majesty's] Subjects and the reputacion of some of the principall persons here, and indeed unhappily clogged and interrupted their Ma'ties affaires which hath been a great vexation to me.*[1]

In May 1693, in an effort to put the colony's troubles in the past and restore a semblance of order and justice, Phips granted pardons to all those still held in the jails. Even those who had escaped confinement by fleeing the colony were pardoned. This meant the fugitives could safely come home and the authorities could begin freeing those who were still behind bars.

More Problems for the Innocent

In spite of the governor's pardons, however, emptying the prisons was not a simple matter. This is because, under the colony's laws, prisoners were financially responsible for their own upkeep while confined in jail. Therefore, only those who could afford it, or whose relatives could afford it, could obtain release. Marion L. Starkey explained,

> *You did not in prison become the guest of the state. [Instead] you paid your way. Even if you were wholly innocent, if it were proved that you had been wrongly deprived of your liberty, you still could not leave until you had reimbursed the jailer for his expenditures in your behalf, the food he had fed you, the shackles he had placed on your wrists and ankles. Prices varied slightly at the various prisons, but in general board averaged about two shillings and sixpence a week. Some of the witches had been running up a bill at this rate*

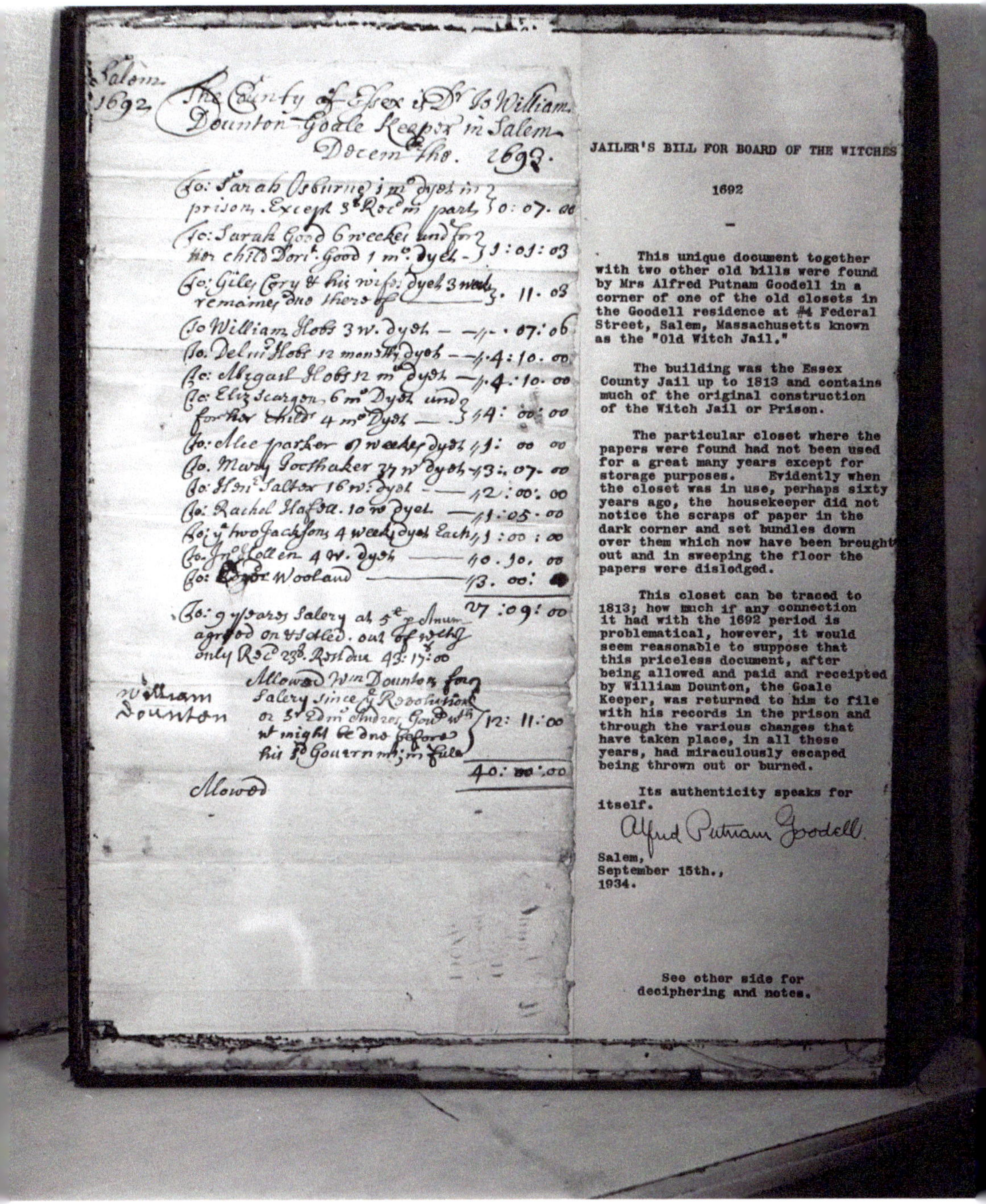
JAILER'S BILL FOR BOARD OF THE WITCHES

1692

This unique document together with two other old bills were found by Mrs Alfred Putnam Goodell in a corner of one of the old closets in the Goodell residence at #4 Federal Street, Salem, Massachusetts known as the "Old Witch Jail."

The building was the Essex County Jail up to 1813 and contains much of the original construction of the Witch Jail or Prison.

The particular closet where the papers were found had not been used for a great many years except for storage purposes. Evidently when the closet was in use, perhaps sixty years ago, the housekeeper did not notice the scraps of paper in the dark corner and set bundles down over them which now have been brought out and in sweeping the floor the papers were dislodged.

This closet can be traced to 1813; how much if any connection it had with the 1692 period is problematical, however, it would seem reasonable to suppose that this priceless document, after being allowed and paid and receipted by William Dounton, the Goale Keeper, was returned to him to file with his records in the prison and through the various changes that have taken place, in all these years, had miraculously escaped being thrown out or burned.

Its authenticity speaks for itself.

Alfred Putnam Goodell

Salem,
September 15th.,
1934.

See other side for deciphering and notes.

Shown here is a document called "Jailer's Bill for Board of the Witches," which was found in a house in Salem in 1949. The house was the former site of the jail where accused witches were imprisoned.

for more than a year … Farms had to be mortgaged to raise the ransom, and they were often farms already impoverished by the half-hearted attention they had had while the trials monopolized everyone's time and attention.[2]

As a result of these unpleasant realities, some people were forced to remain in jail well after they had been pardoned. Inmate Mary Watkins managed to get out only after a Virginia planter paid her prison bills in exchange for her working for several years as his indentured servant. Meanwhile, another imprisoned woman, Margaret Jacobs, had the good fortune to have a kindly local citizen pay her way to freedom; she was expected to pay him back, but only at a rate that she could manage comfortably. Sadly, a few people died in jail because they simply had no way to pay and no friends or family who could help them.

Though the trials ended and the prisons eventually emptied, justice was not immediately served in the cases of most who had been drawn into the nightmare of witchcraft panic. However, that did not stop many of these wronged people from seeking justice, even when it took years to achieve it. In 1693, not long after Governor Phips issued his pardons, several of the released prisoners applied to the colonial government to get back their confiscated property. These petitions were ignored at first, but the injured parties persisted. Eventually, a few people were given their property and legal rights back; for example, Elizabeth Proctor petitioned to have her rights restored, such as her right to inherit money. As someone who had been found guilty in court in Puritan times, those rights were originally stripped from her, leaving her with no way to get the money that legally belonged to her.

Her rights were restored slowly and mostly through her efforts to petition the government. In 1697, she was allowed to inherit her dowry, which was money a bride brought to the marriage. Essentially, a husband was meant to use a dowry to keep his wife well cared for, and it gave the wife financial security if her husband died. In 1702, the Massachusetts General Court declared the trials unlawful, and in 1703, a bill was passed that reversed the decision against Elizabeth Proctor as well as her husband and

Rebecca Nurse. This meant Elizabeth could file a claim to get her husband's property back.

In 1709, many of the people who had suffered because of the trials submitted a petition calling for the legal reversal of all convictions in the witch trials, including those of the people who had been executed. Finally, in 1711, a bill passed reversing all the former convictions. The government also gave financial compensation to the families of 23 of the victims.

Aftermath and Consequences

When the witch trials ended, they weren't just forgiven and forgotten. The people of Salem and the surrounding towns had spent the better part of a year living in an atmosphere of suspicion and terror. Anyone could be accused at any time, and some people actually believed that people they had known all their lives were secretly witches who deserved to be put to death. Even after Governor Phips put a stop to the arrests and trials, the accusers and hundreds of the accused were still living together.

With much disdain and anger, many of the victims and their families remembered the key role played by Reverend Parris, who had stirred up much of the hysteria through his incendiary sermons warning that witches lurked at every turn. They also remembered the roles played by the judges who had often allowed their decisions to rest entirely on spectral evidence—which relied solely on taking the word of one person over another, since it could never be scientifically proven. Additionally, there were the roles played by the accusers, who had indirectly caused the deaths of innocent people. It seemed only fair that these individuals should have to pay some kind of price for their failings.

In some cases, the key perpetrators did suffer some kind of negative consequences. In the months following the end of the trials, for instance, Reverend Parris encountered the wrath of many in his congregation who held him partly responsible for the witch hunt. Early in 1697, a group of these Salem Village churchgoers attempted to void his salary. "His believing the devil's accusations," they said, "and readily departing from all charity to persecute the

Samuel Sewall was the only Salem judge to apologize for his part in the witch trials.

blameless and godly [citizens] are just causes for our refusal [to pay him]."[3] Parris fought back for a while, but over time, more and more villagers refused to set foot in church while he was still the minister. Later in 1697, he finally resigned and left town, taking Betty with him. The new village minister, Joseph Green, eventually restored order in the church and reinstated Rebecca Nurse, Giles Corey, and others whom Parris had expelled at the height of witchcraft hysteria. Although they were already dead, Puritans believed it was important for them to be part of the church if their souls were to go to heaven. Had they still been alive, this would have been a very meaningful action to them.

Most of the judges who had served in the Court of Oyer and Terminer did not suffer the kind of social rejection that Reverend Parris did. However, one of them, Samuel Sewall, did end up apologizing for his role in the tragedy. In January 1697, Sewall released a statement that a local minister recited from the pulpit. It read in part, "Samuel Sewall … as to the Guilt contracted, upon the opening of the late Commission of Oyer and Terminer at Salem … Desires to take the Blame and Shame of it, Asking pardon of Men, And especially desiring prayers that God … would pardon that sin and all his other sins."[4]

As for the young girls whose actions had largely driven the witch hunt, most were never punished for causing such misery. A few—including Betty Parris, Mercy Lewis, and Mary Walcott—did eventually marry, although little is known about their later lives. Only one of the girls, Ann Putnam Jr., publicly expressed remorse for what she had done. In 1706, she wrote a confession and gave it to Reverend Green to read to his congregation in Salem Village. "I desire to be humbled before God," it began,

> *for that sad and humbling providence that befell my father's family in the year about '92; that I, then being in my childhood, should, by such a providence of God, be made an instrument for the accusing of several persons of a grievous crime, whereby their lives were taken away from them, whom now I have just grounds and good reason to believe they were innocent persons; and that it was a great delusion of Satan*

that deceived me in that sad time, whereby I justly fear I have been instrumental, with others, though ignorantly and unwittingly, to bring upon myself and this land the guilt of innocent blood ... Particularly, as I was a chief instrument of accusing of Goodwife Nurse and her two sisters, I desire to lie in the dust, and to be humbled for it, in that I was a cause, with others, of so sad a calamity to them and their families; for which ... [I] earnestly beg forgiveness of God, and from all those unto whom I have given just cause of sorrow and offence.[5]

The members of Reverend Green's congregation generously forgave her and allowed her to join them. However, there were many in Salem, including some who had lived through the witch hunt and their children born later, who refused to accept such apologies after the fact. In their view, repentance, though admirable, could not bring back dead loved ones or restore ruined family reputations.

One example was Philip English, a Salem merchant whose wife, Mary, had been accused of witchcraft, dragged from her bed, and thrown into jail. She escaped execution and was later released, but for decades following the trials, English loudly denounced all the former authority figures who had run them, including the Reverend Nicholas Noyes. His anger over the treatment of his wife and the brutal, untimely deaths of his friends John Proctor and Rebecca Nurse never subsided. On his deathbed in 1736, English was urged finally to forgive Noyes, who had died several years before, but he took his grudge to the grave.

Understanding What Happened

The enduring legacy of the Salem witch trials is what they taught us about the danger of letting fear become stronger than reason, especially in matters of government and law. At times throughout American history, hysteria has led to injustice, especially for minority groups. When this happens, the memory of the Salem witch trials is sometimes invoked to remind people of what can happen when we let false accusations rooted in fear ruin innocent lives.

The McCarthy hearings are perhaps the best-known example of a modern American witch hunt, but they are far from the only example. Controversial stop and frisk laws, which allow law enforcement officials to stop and search anyone they think looks threatening, ultimately target black and Latino men more than any other group. Many call the practice a kind of modern witch hunt rooted in the false fear that people of these races are more prone to violent action. In addition, following the terrorist attacks of September 11, 2001, many Muslims living in the United States were the victims of false accusations and irrational suspicion.

In times of fear and uncertainty, our first instinct is often to look for people to punish and blame—and those who are different than us are easy targets, just as Tituba was for the Puritans. It is easy to give in to hysteria, but the Salem witch trials taught us that this way leads to chaos and injustice. Americans must continue to learn from the dark events of the past, such as the Salem witch trials, and work hard to ensure that history does not repeat itself.

Today, most people don't believe witchcraft is real. Witches are the subject of many popular fictional books, TV shows, and movies, including the best-selling *Harry Potter* series. Some of these depict witches and magic in a fun, fantasy way, where people do instantaneous magic with almost no effort. Others show witches the way they've typically been viewed in the past: performing blood sacrifices, worshipping Satan, and harming people. While many people think these fictional depictions of witches are fun and harmless, some conservative Christians do still believe that witchcraft is real and dangerous, and these people have a religious objection to it. People with this view may refuse to read *Harry Potter* or watch shows such as Netflix's *The Chilling Adventures of Sabrina*. Some people have claimed that reciting the spells in *Harry Potter* has caused things to happen in real life, but these claims have never been proven.

There are also people who call themselves witches in real life, but they're very different than either of these two fictional depictions. According to the website Gaia, modern witchcraft "is simply about using the power of the universe and the mind to attract

wants and desires."[6] People who consider themselves witches use spells to achieve goals, such as bringing themselves luck, or to worship the gods or goddesses they believe in. When some people hear the word "spells," they think of things they may have seen in horror movies, but witches don't sacrifice people or drink blood. Generally, spells involve harmless activities such as lighting candles of specific colors, burning specific herbs, and reciting certain words. They can be performed alone or with others, similar to the way someone who follows a more traditional religion can either pray alone or attend a church service.

People who have different beliefs sometimes view modern-day witches with suspicion or exasperation, but rarely are they

People who call themselves witches use items such as herbs, candles, and crystals in their religious practices. Modern-day witches bear no resemblance to the Puritan concept of a witch.

persecuted anymore, and anyone who tried to bring a case of bewitchment before a court would be dismissed immediately. However, this doesn't mean people have stopped irrationally blaming others for things they haven't done. In recent years, immigrants—especially people from Mexico—have been vilified and accused of things such as stealing jobs from Americans, committing violent acts, and draining the country's financial resources. In reality, these accusations almost never turn out to be true. Remembering the Salem witch trials and the way people in power ignored evidence in favor of finding guilt provides an important lesson that people in the 21st century should take to heart.

How You See History

1. Why did the witch trials stop gradually instead of all at once?
2. How do you think you would feel after the witch trials ended if you had been living in Salem at the time?
3. Describe a current situation in which a particular group is treated unfairly. What lessons from the Salem witch trials can you apply to this situation?

January 1692

Betty Parris and Abigail Williams begin displaying strange behavior.

February 24, 1692

Dr. William Griggs announces that the cause of the girls' fits is witchcraft.

February 25, 1692

Mary Sibley encourages Tituba and John Indian to bake a witch cake.

February 26, 1692

Abigail and Betty accuse Tituba.

February 27, 1692

Ann Putnam Jr. and Elizabeth Hubbard start having fits and accuse Sarah Good and Sarah Osborne.

March 1, 1692

Tituba, Sarah Good, and Sarah Osborne are questioned; Tituba confesses.

March 23, 1692

Rebecca Nurse is arrested; John Proctor publicly denounces the accusers.

March 29, 1692

Elizabeth and John Proctor are accused by Abigail Williams and Mercy Lewis.

April 11, 1692

Elizabeth Proctor and Sarah Cloyce are questioned; John Proctor defends his wife and is accused by Mary Warren and subsequently arrested.

May 27, 1692

Governor Phips appoints several men to a Court of Oyer and Terminer.

June 2, 1692
The court holds its first session.

June 10, 1692
Bridget Bishop is executed.

June 29–30, 1692
Rebecca Nurse is found not guilty, but protests force the jury to change its verdict.

August 19, 1692
John Proctor, George Burroughs, George Jacobs Sr., John Willard, and Martha Carrier are hanged; Rebecca Eames is accused of witchcraft at the hanging, is arrested and questioned that day, and pleads guilty while accusing her son.

September 17–19, 1692
Giles Corey is pressed to death.

October 29, 1692
Governor Phips orders an end to all arrests and dissolves the Court of Oyer and Terminer.

November 25, 1692
Governor Phips establishes a Superior Court of Judicature, which outlaws spectral evidence, to determine whether anyone left in jail is guilty.

May 1693
Governor Phips officially pardons everyone left in jail and formally ends the witch trials.

NOTES

Introduction: A Misunderstood Event

1. Tara Isabella Burton, "There Weren't Any Witches in Salem in 1693. But There Sure Are Now," Vox, October 30, 2017, www.vox.com/identities/2017/10/30/16560092/salem-witch-trials-magic-halloween-witchcraft-arthur-miller-crucible-past.
2. Burton, "There Weren't Any Witches."

Chapter One: Setting the Stage

1. Jeff Wallenfeldt, "Salem Witch Trials," *Encyclopedia Britannica*, modified July 18, 2019, www.britannica.com/event/Salem-witch-trials.
2. Quoted in Rebecca Beatrice Brooks, "Reverend Samuel Parris: Was He to Blame for the Salem Witch Trials?," *History of Massachusetts* (blog), September 8, 2015, historyofmassachusetts.org/reverend-samuel-parris.
3. N. Carr, "Socio-Political Causes," The Salem Witch Trials, December 4, 2016, wludh.ca/dh100/2016/T4/G5/M1/causes/socio-political-causes.

Chapter Two: The Incidents Start

1. "Colonial Women: Rebecca Greensmith," *History of American Women* (blog), accessed September 11, 2019, www.womenhistoryblog.com/2008/03/rebecca-greensmith.html.
2. Quoted in "Increase Mather: Remarkable Providences: An Essay for the Recording of Illustrious Providences (Boston, 1684)," Hanover Historical Texts Project, accessed September 26, 2019, history.hanover.edu/texts/matherrp.html.
3. Rebecca Beatrice Brooks, "Tituba: The Slave of Salem," *History of Massachusetts* (blog), January 2, 2013, historyofmassachusetts.org/tituba-the-slave-of-salem.
4. Quoted in Rebecca Beatrice Brooks, "What Caused the Salem Witch Trials?," *History of Massachusetts* (blog), June 30, 2018, historyofmassachusetts.org/salem-witch-trials-causes.
5. N. Carr, "Ergotism," The Salem Witch Trials, accessed September 27, 2019, wludh.ca/dh100/2016/T4/G5/M1/causes/ergotism.

Chapter Three: Accusations and Trials

1. Jone Johnson Lewis, "Salem Witch Trials Timeline," ThoughtCo., modified September 17, 2019, www.thoughtco.com/salem-witch-trials-timeline-3530778.
2. Marion L. Starkey, *The Devil in Massachusetts: A Modern Enquiry into the Salem Witch Trials* (New York, NY: Random House, 1989), p. 51.
3. Stacy Schiff, *The Witches: Salem, 1692* (New York, NY: Little, Brown and Company, 2015), p. 49.
4. Quoted in Marilynne K. Roach, *The Salem Witch Trials: A Day-by-Day Chronicle of a Community Under Siege* (New York, NY: Taylor Trade, 2002), p. 31.
5. Quoted in Frances Hill, ed., *The Salem Witch Trials Reader* (New York, NY: Da Capo, 2000), p. 62.
6. Jeff Wallenfeldt, "Salem Witch Trials," *Encyclopedia Britannica*, modified July 18, 2019, www.britannica.com/event/Salem-witch-trials.
7. Wallenfeldt, "Salem Witch Trials."
8. Evan Andrews, "7 Bizarre Witch Trial Tests," History.com, modified September 1, 2018, www.history.com/news/7-bizarre-witch-trial-tests.
9. Jone Johnson Lewis, "Bridget Bishop," ThoughtCo., modified March 13, 2019, www.thoughtco.com/bridget-bishop-biography-3530330.

Chapter Four: Innocent People Killed

1. Quoted in Frances Hill, ed., *The Salem Witch Trials Reader* (New York, NY: Da Capo, 2000), p. 77.
2. Quoted in Hill, *The Salem Witch Trials Reader*, pp. 77–78.
3. Quoted in "SWP No. 024: Martha Carrier Executed, August 19, 1692," Salem Witch Trials Documentary Archive and Transcription Project, accessed October 1, 2019, salem.lib.virginia.edu/n24.html.
4. Quoted in Marilynne K. Roach, *The Salem Witch Trials: A Day-by-Day Chronicle of a Community Under Siege* (New York, NY: Taylor Trade, 2002), p. 227.
5. Quoted in Rebecca Beatrice Brooks, "The Curse of Giles Corey," *History of Massachusetts* (blog), October 12, 2011, historyofmassachusetts.org/the-curse-of-giles-corey.

Chapter Five: The End of the Panic

1. Quoted in George Lincoln Burr, ed., *Narratives of the Witchcraft Cases, 1648–1706* (New York, NY: Charles Scribner's Sons, 1914), p. 201.
2. Marion L. Starkey, *The Devil in Massachusetts: A Modern Enquiry into the Salem Witch Trials* (New York, NY: Random House, 1989), p. 230.
3. Quoted in Starkey, *The Devil in Massachusetts*, p. 250.
4. "The Diary of Samuel Sewall, 1674–1729," Salem Witch Trials Documentary Archive and Transcription Project, accessed October 4, 2019, salem.lib.virginia.edu/diaries/sewall_diary.html.
5. Quoted in Rebecca Beatrice Brooks, "Ann Putnam, Jr: Villain or Victim?," *History of Massachusetts* (blog), July 6, 2015, historyofmassachusetts.org/ann-putnam-jr.
6. Laurie Rihiimaki, "What Does It Mean to Be a Witch?," Gaia, February 11, 2019, www.gaia.com/article/what-does-it-mean-to-be-a-witch.

FOR MORE INFORMATION

Books: Nonfiction

Boraas, Tracey. *The Salem Witch Trials*. Mankato, MN: Capstone, 2003.

Landau, Elaine. *The Salem Witchcraft Trials: Would You Join the Madness?* Berkeley Heights, NJ: Enslow Elementary, 2015.

Ohlin, Nancy, and Roger Simó. *The Salem Witch Trials*. New York, NY: Little Bee Books, 2017.

Rice, Dona. *Unsolved! History's Mysteries*. Bainbridge Island, WA: Triangle Interactive, 2018.

Schanzer, Rosalyn. *Witches!: The Absolutely True Tale of Disaster in Salem*. Washington, DC: National Geographic, 2011.

Books: Fiction

Miller, Arthur. *The Crucible*. Oxford, UK: Oxford University Press, 2019.

Speare, Elizabeth George. *The Witch of Blackbird Pond*. New York, NY: Houghton Mifflin Harcourt, 1958.

Websites

Investigating Power: McCarthyism
investigatingpower.org/mccarthyism
This website examines the Red Scare "witch hunts" and how Joseph McCarthy gained so much power.

***National Geographic*: Salem Witch Trials**
nationalgeographic.org/interactive/salem-interactive
This interactive website explains the trials' history while also giving visitors an opportunity to engage with the material through games and quizzes.

Salem Witch Museum: Kids' Questions
salemwitchmuseum.com/video-categories/kids-questions
Alison D'Amario, director of education at the Salem Witch Museum in Salem, Massachusetts, answers questions about the Salem witch trials submitted by real kids.

Salem Witch Trials Documentary Archive and Transcription Project
salem.lib.virginia.edu/home.html
This collection of primary documents gives a deeper understanding of the Salem witch trials.

***Smithsonian*: A Brief History of the Salem Witch Trials**
www.smithsonianmag.com/history/a-brief-history-of-the-salem-witch-trials-175162489
This website provides a simplified history of the trials with concrete information and interesting images.

INDEX

PHOTO CREDITS

Cover, pp. 58–59 Bettmann/Bettmann/Getty Images; p. 4 Morphart Creation/Shutterstock.com; pp. 8–9 Joseph Prezioso/AFP/Getty Images; p. 10 Stock Montage/Getty Images; p. 14 Courtesy of the Library of Congress; pp. 16–17 DEA/Biblioteca Ambrosiana/De Agostini/Getty Images; p. 19 Interim Archives/Getty Images; p. 22 General Photographic Agency/Getty Images; pp. 24–25 Alexander Erdbeer/Shutterstock.com; pp. 28–29, 52–53, 70–71 Universal History Archive/Universal Images Group via Getty Images; pp. 32–33 Manfred Ruckszio/Shutterstock.com; p. 36 © iStockphoto.com/littleny; p. 40 © Historical Picture Archive/Corbis/Corbis via Getty Images; pp. 42–43, 86 Everett Historical/Shutterstock.com; pp. 44–45 schubbel/Shutterstock.com; pp. 48–49 The Print Collector/Getty Images; pp. 54–55 Tom Tom/Shutterstock.com; pp. 60, 74, 83 Nina Leen/The LIFE Picture Collection via Getty Images; pp. 64–65 John Tlumacki/The Boston Globe via Getty Images; p. 81 Education Images/Universal Images Group via Getty Images; pp. 90–91 Vera Petruk/Shutterstock.com.

ABOUT THE AUTHOR

Donna Reynolds is a freelance writer and editor who has worked on more than 50 books for young adults. She has a degree in English from the University of Wisconsin–Madison and spends as much time as possible traveling around the world. She tries to volunteer at a local nonprofit organization at least one day a week, no matter where she happens to be.